REASSESSING THE INCUMBENCY EFFECT

Incumbents in the U.S. House of Representatives have presumably increased their vote percentages in recent decades, raising questions about the efficacy of elections in making members responsive. The evidence, however, indicates there has been no improvement in the electoral fortunes of incumbents in the last 50 years. Only Republicans have improved their electoral fortunes, as a result of realignment. This valuable book provides a very different interpretation of how incumbents have fared in recent decades, and the interpretation is supported by nontechnical data analysis and presentation.

Jeffrey M. Stonecash is Maxwell Professor in the Department of Political Science, The Maxwell School, Syracuse University. He researches political parties, changes in their electoral bases, and how these changes affect political polarization and public policy debates. His recent books are *Class and Party in American Politics* (2000), *Diverging Parties* (2003), *Parties Matter* (2005), *Split: Class and Cultural Divides in American Politics* (2007), and *Political Polling, Second Edition* (2008). He is now working with Mark Brewer on a book about the dynamics of party realignment since 1900. He has done polling and consulting for political candidates since 1985.

Reassessing the Incumbency Effect

Jeffrey M. Stonecash

Syracuse University

CAMBRIDGE
UNIVERSITY PRESS

CAMBRIDGE UNIVERSITY PRESS
Cambridge, New York, Melbourne, Madrid, Cape Town, Singapore, São Paulo, Delhi

Cambridge University Press
32 Avenue of the Americas, New York, NY 10013-2473, USA

www.cambridge.org
Information on this title: www.cambridge.org/9780521733229

© Jeffrey M. Stonecash 2008

First published 2008

Printed in the United States of America

A catalog record for this publication is available from the British Library.

Library of Congress Cataloging in Publication Data

Stonecash, Jeffrey M.
Reassessing the incumbency effect / Jeffrey M. Stonecash.
    p.   cm.
Includes bibliographical references and index.
ISBN 978-0-521-51551-1 (hardback) – ISBN 978-0-521-73322-9 (pbk.)
1. Incumbency (Public officers) – United States.   2. Elections – United States.
I. Title.
JK1965.S76   2008
324.973–dc22   2008014098

ISBN   978-0-521-51551-1 hardback
ISBN   978-0-521-73322-9 paperback

To Kathryn

Contents

PART III: APPENDICES: MORE DETAILED ANALYSES OF
INCUMBENCY EFFECT INDICATORS

Preface

It is widely presumed that, in recent decades, House incumbents have been able to increase their vote percentages. Incumbents have always had an advantage over challengers. The argument is that this advantage has increased. The implications of this conclusion for democracy are troubling. It raises issues about the fairness of elections and the responsiveness of legislators. Incumbents may be able to exploit the advantages of office, boost their vote percentages, and become more electorally secure. That, in turn, may make them less responsive to voters and changes in public opinion.

This book challenges the conclusion that the electoral fortunes of incumbents have improved. It then presents an alternative interpretation of the trends that have occurred. The argument of this book is that the evidence presented to support this conclusion does not hold up to reanalysis. Incumbents as a group have not experienced an increase in their vote percentages. Other indicators of incumbent fortunes, to be reviewed in later chapters, also do not support the conclusion that is so often presented. Furthermore, the quantitative statistical analyses of the incumbency effect that have been presented to support the conclusion are fatally flawed.

Not only does the evidence of an increased incumbency effect fail to hold up, but the focus on all incumbents leads us away from a more relevant interpretation of change. There was change in the mid-1960s, but it involved a significant and sustained improvement in the fortunes of only Republican House members. The shift that took place beginning in the 1960s can best be seen as reflecting a partisan secular realignment helping Republican incumbents.

These very divergent conclusions – a general rise in the incumbency advantage versus it being only for one party – reflect very different understandings of partisanship in American politics. Much of the increased incumbency effect interpretation is based on the conclusion that the partisan attachments of voters are declining. Incumbents are seen as reacting to and exploiting that change to create more candidate-centered campaigns, in which the attachment is to them and not to a party. The alternative interpretation presented here suggests that the changes occurring in the 1960s and 1970s were the beginning of a sustained secular realignment that has been partisan in nature. Voters were sorting themselves out between the two parties and not moving away from parties. The increased incumbency effect argument assumes dealignment; however, it is really realignment unfolding.

These alternative interpretations also involve very different normative implications. The conclusion that the incumbency effect is increasing is accompanied by concerns that the increase is a result of members exploiting public resources. They send too much mail to their constituents, issue too many press releases, get too many paid trips to their districts, and stick too many pork-barrel projects into budget bills in Congress to please local constituents. They are also raising too much in campaign funds, discouraging challengers, and becoming too tied to contributors. The presumption is that representation is at risk. In stark contrast, if change reflects a partisan shift of voters from one party to the other, then change might be seen as part of a normal process of voters realigning their voting allegiances to reflect altered preferences. Representation is not at risk but rather is occurring through the process of voters moving to support the party candidates seen as most desirable to them.

The first goal of this book is to prompt a reexamination of an important conclusion about American elections. The analyses that have been presented to support an increased incumbency effect conclusion have significant limitations and need to be reassessed. If prior analyses do not hold up to scrutiny, the conclusion about an increased incumbency effect needs to be discarded.

This is not to argue that, in any given year, incumbents do not have an advantage versus challengers. As will be discussed later, incumbents generally have greater visibility, more campaign funds, and access to numerous public resources to promote themselves. Money and the ability to engage in promotion matter, and always will. Incumbents win at a high rate, and that has persisted. The issue is whether that advantage has increased over time, which involves changes over time and not situations within any given year.

The second goal of this book is to establish another view of the changes that happened in the 1960s and generate additional research to explain what happened. This analysis is only a start on more detailed analyses. We need research that focuses on why Republicans made such gains in 1966 and why they maintained those gains in subsequent elections. This analysis outlines the nature of the partisan change that occurred in recent decades and suggests where we need to concentrate our attention.

The analysis is far from exhaustive in explaining the shifts that occurred. It presents the need for a reassessment and provides an alternative framework, but finding out exactly why and how change happened when it did will require more detailed analyses. The last chapter explores the issues that will require further analysis. While the analysis is by no means complete, the first step is to change how the patterns of recent decades are seen. If that can be achieved, then research efforts will eventually tell us what happened. The hope is that this book prompts that first step.

THE PLAN OF THE BOOK

The book is organized into three main sections. Chapters 1 and 2 introduce the issue, the presumed change, its significance, and the development of a consensus about an increased incumbency effect. The second section involves a reexamination of the data, with a focus on whether the data justify the conclusions reached. If the conventional wisdom is to be reassessed, there has to be a basis for discarding the conclusion that there has been an increase. Chapter 3 reconsiders the much-discussed vote percentage of incumbents from 1946 to 2006. Chapter 4 examines the net ability of incumbents to increase their vote percentages over their careers, and then Chapter 5 assesses the retirement slump.

While there has not been a general increase in the fortunes of incumbents in recent decades, something did happen in the mid-1960s. The explanation presented here is that the change that did occur involved only Republicans. This alternative explanation of change is introduced in Chapter 6, which focuses on the long-term, gradual changes in the fortunes of the parties. Then Chapter 7 applies that framework to reinterpret the trends that have received so much attention. Chapter 8 addresses the implications of the results of our assessment of American politics.

Finally, many may still wonder how an explanation that stresses partisan shifts over time can coexist with several analyses that seem to rather convincingly demonstrate that the incumbency effect increased from the 1950s until now. Some of the analyses that indicate an increasing incumbency effect or an increasing retirement slump are fairly complicated, quantitative, and deserve more detailed analyses. Appendix A examines, in some detail, changes in the retirement slump indicator, and Appendix B reviews the Gelman-King analysis; these appendices are intended for those who would like a more extensive analysis of the limits of these efforts to track changes in the incumbency effect.

Acknowledgments

This is a project that has taken a long time. The major challenge was in creating an accurate data file of House elections. I am greatly indebted to two students who displayed remarkable work ethics and persistence in helping me do that. We began with existing Inter-University Consortium for Political and Social Research data files and then checked every record to make sure it was correct. We did that using Michael Dubin's (1998) *United States Congressional Elections, 1788–1997*. We then added in special elections and losers as a separate file so there would be a record for every winner and loser. We also corrected and updated John Hibbing's file on biographical data, including when members entered and left. Peter Neuberger, who has gone on to study medicine, did a remarkable job calmly checking every number. I was impressed by and very grateful for his patience with and care for this endeavor. Every faculty member should have an assistant like Peter.

Then all files were merged, and the process of checking to see if everything merged correctly began. We checked all results and all incumbency coding. The challenge, then, was why certain records were wrong and what should be done with cases that did not fit conventional patterns. A socialist in Milwaukee was elected numerous times but never seated because Congress refused to seat a socialist. Was he an incumbent, even though he never sat in the House? We decided that the answer is yes because he was the prior winner and no one was elected in a special election. Patsy Mink from Hawaii was reelected to Congress several months after she died. Can the reelection of a deceased person count? We decided it does. Voters have a right to reelect whomever they wish. How do you code a person elected in November both to fill out a vacant seat for the rest of the year and to serve for the next full term? The issues were fascinating and often difficult. Joe Brichacek did a remarkable job pursuing errors, inconsistencies, and missing information. It became a challenge to resolve all problems by his graduation, but he did so. He was another rare assistant, and I thank him very much. He is now in political consulting and doing well.

There are probably still some errors in the data set used for this analysis, but the accuracy that does exist could never have been achieved without the dedication of Peter and Joe. I am grateful.

PART I

An Increased Incumbency Effect: Reconsidering Evidence

CHAPTER 1

An Increased Incumbency Effect
and American Politics

Incumbents have always fared well against challengers. Indeed, it would be surprising if those in office did not do better on average than those unelected. The important matter is that this advantage has reportedly increased in recent decades. Numerous studies indicate that beginning in the 1960s, incumbents were able to win more frequently and increase their vote percentages. Incumbents have always had a high success rate versus challengers, and now they do even better.

Specific trends will be examined later, but several changes indicate how members of Congress have been able to change the electoral landscape. Members are now able to increase their vote percentages from their first to their second elections more than in the past. The average percentage of the vote incumbents receive is now greater than in the 1940s and 1950s. More incumbents are elected with more than 60 percent of the vote, a common hurdle to achieve a safe seat. Members of the House are now able to stay in office longer than in the early 1900s. From the 1940s through the 1970s, the correlation of their electoral vote to the presidential vote in their district declined, reducing the threat of loss from a national swing in sentiment against one party. They were able to disconnect their vote from the president's vote. It became increasingly common for scholars and commentators to note that the *incumbency effect* was powerful and growing.

There also appears to be a very plausible explanation of why the incumbency effect has increased. The growth of federal programs provided incumbents with more resources to deliver to their districts.

They also have more resources to promote themselves and remind voters of all the good things they are doing. Since the 1950s, incumbents in the Congress have voted themselves larger staffs so they can engage in more contact with voters. These larger staffs allow members to help constituents with personal problems, which can create gratitude among voters. Larger staffs and budgets mean members can send more newsletters to constituents and press releases to media outlets, increasing their visibility to voters. Members now have greater allowances for travel back and forth to the district, providing them with more opportunities to visit local groups, hear the groups' concerns, and explain their own positions. All these activities involve using increases in public resources to curry favor with the electorate and increase the member's positive image before the electorate. Incumbents also are raising more campaign funds, which allow them to buy campaign ads to present themselves to voters, boosting their name recognition and intimidating possible challengers. In short, members now have more opportunities to do things for their districts and the resources to tell voters what they have done. Finding evidence that the vote percentages of incumbents are increasing should not be surprising.

These changes in the electoral fortunes of incumbents have not been well received by critics, who have offered four main arguments about how the growing incumbency effect is bad for democracy. First, some are very troubled by the steady increase in the use of public tax dollars to fund self-promotional activities such as letters, newsletters, press releases, and government-funded appearances at local events (Mayhew, 1974b; Jacobson, 2001: 30–32). They are also troubled by the practice of adding numerous pork-barrel projects to the federal budget so the local member can look good to constituents (Fiorina, 1977a, 1977b). They see the extensive use of public resources as an inappropriate exploitation of public tax dollars for the promotion of individual careers.

Perhaps the more compelling criticisms involve the negative effects on democracy and responsiveness. The second argument is that the focus within offices on promoting members reduces the focus on issues. Members can presumably use all these resources to increase their visibility and create a "personal" connection with voters, one based less on issues and partisan inclinations and more on good feelings toward the individual member. This reduces the role of issues and policy votes in voting decisions. Elections, which should presumably focus on policy issues, become more of a personal referendum.

Third, the greater visibility of incumbents also makes it harder for challengers to mount a campaign against them. This in turn reduces their anxiety about the next election. If competition – the prospect of a relatively close election – makes an incumbent pay close attention to district constituents, the expectation of relatively high vote percentages for incumbents will likely diminish that attention. The safer incumbents feel, the less attention they are likely to give to the district, reducing representation and responsiveness (MacRae, 1952; Froman, 1963b; Fiorina, 1973; Griffin, 2006).

Fourth, the greater the increase in the incumbency effect, the less likely it will be that swings in public sentiment will register in Congress. If the electorate dislikes the policies being enacted, but a growing percentage of incumbents are safe, then fewer incumbents will be ousted in an election. Changes in public sentiment are less likely to translate into shifts in party dominance, and responsiveness will decline. Put simply, if Democrats or Republicans control Congress and enact policies disliked by many Americans, and if most representatives of the majority party are safe, they may be able to enact such policies with impunity. To critics, the growth of the incumbency effect has not been a desirable development.

These conclusions about the advantages incumbents enjoy have now become part of the portrait of American politics presented to students. Incumbents are now reported to be safer than in the past (Herrnson, 2004: 30–68; Jacobson, 2004: 23–51). Texts on American politics report to students that "the reelection rate is astonishingly high" (Janda, Berry, and Goldman, 2005: 341). "The best thing a candidate can have going for him or her is simply to be the incumbent" (Edwards, Wattenberg, and Lineberry, 2004: 359). Texts either suggest that change has occurred – "the incredible incumbency advantage enjoyed by modern-day House members" (Wilson and Dilulio, 2006: 235) – or state it more explicitly – "Incumbents have always had an advantage, but critics point to recent changes that have made matters worse" (Shea, Green, and Smith, 2007: 557–58). The larger and more important consequence is the impact on the political process. Incumbents "normally win easily. An effect is to reduce Congress's responsiveness to political change" (Patterson, 2006: 366). "The advantage of incumbency thus tends to preserve the status quo in Congress" (Ginsberg, Lowi, and Weir, 2005: 478).

Members of Congress are central actors in democracy. They are the ones who seek to understand and represent constituencies. We presume that the process of seeking reelection prompts them to be sensitive to public concerns and responsive to voters. If public and private resources are creating a process whereby challengers are discouraged and incumbents are systematically less attentive and less responsive, there are reasons to worry about the health of democracy. If these endeavors are successful, incumbents can insulate themselves from voter sentiment and reduce their responsiveness to their district electorate (Burnham, 1975).

The sense that incumbents are manipulating the process and blocking responsiveness and change has prompted efforts to constrain the incumbency effect. During the 1990s a strong movement to limit the terms of state legislators developed, driven in part by a sense that incumbents were unresponsive and out of touch and needed to be removed. The courts have ruled that members of Congress cannot be term-limited, so critics have argued that congressional budgets should be cut back and that there should be stronger limits on the extent to which members can mail constituents at public expense.

DOUBTS ABOUT FINDINGS AND INTERPRETATION

The evidence that the incumbency effect increased after the 1940s seems clear. But what if the incumbency effect has not actually increased? Incumbents have always had an advantage over challengers. The issue is whether this advantage has increased. What if the evidence does not justify the accepted conclusions? What if there has not been a change in the ability of incumbents to boost their vote percentages? If change has not occurred, a vaguely negative and inaccurate view of the nature of elections has been presented, and a considerable amount of skepticism about elections and incumbents is without foundation.

Why reconsider this general conclusion, given the accumulation of studies documenting it? The process by which we reconsider established conclusions is often less than systematic. In my case the prompt to take another look at the evidence involving this issue emerged by chance. I was working on an analysis of realignment in House elections for another book (Stonecash, Brewer, and Mariani, 2003). As a part of the analysis, I was trying to re-create the often-reported increase in the average percentage of the vote received by incumbents since 1946. Despite repeated efforts to find that increase, I was consistently finding an essentially flat trend or no increase over time. After checking to make sure that the data and computer program were correct, I carefully reread the literature that produced the conclusion that there has been an upward trend. The footnotes of those works explained, without much justification, that all cases in which a House candidate was unopposed by a major party candidate were deleted.

This means that portrayals of elections over time for the House of Representatives did not involve all House elections. That prompted questions about how many cases (districts) were being deleted, how the number had changed over time, and whether variations over time in the number of districts included had any impact on the reported trend in the average percentage of the vote incumbents receive. The answers were intriguing.

During the 1950s, there were 70–90 seats uncontested by a major party (Democrat or Republican), and that number dropped to 40–50 in the early 1960s, just when the incumbency advantage was reported to increase. This meant that the number of cases was shifting over time and that districts previously uncompetitive were being added to the analysis. It also suggested the puzzling possibility that at the very time competition was reported to be declining, more districts were becoming contested.

The important matter is the empirical effect of the interplay between which districts are included in the analysis and the average vote of incumbents. If uncontested districts are excluded, there is an increase over time in the average vote percentage. If all districts are included, there is no increase. It seemed odd to me that both of these conclusions were not part of the portrait of House elections, rather than just the former. Perhaps the presumed increase was not quite so clear. This realization made me wonder if it would be worthwhile to reexamine the other standard indicators of the incumbency effect. It appeared that acceptance of the approach to calculating the incumbency effect – deleting uncontested races – was rather uncritical. Someone had done so initially, and it became conventional practice without any debate. Perhaps there were problems with the other indicators, and the trend results of other indicators also needed to be reconsidered. And, as will be examined in subsequent pages, that review indicates that the presumption that these indicators support the claim of an increased incumbency effect should also be seen with considerable skepticism.

Not only were there reasons to reconsider the existence of certain trends, but there were also reasons to wonder if existing trends might be better explained by another framework. The underlying premise of the growing-incumbency-effect approach is that the electorate is becoming less attached to parties and that effective members of Congress can exploit that to create a so-called personal vote and increase their vote percentages. But American politics is becoming increasingly partisan, and party identification is increasing (Stonecash, 2006; Jacobson, 2007). Furthermore, Republicans abruptly took over the House in 1994 and held it for some time, suggesting that their fortunes had improved. Partisanship was on the rise, and Republicans seemed to be benefiting the most from this. I then realized that I had never seen the trend in *safe seats* (defined as a member who receives 60 percent or more of the vote) presented by party. The original analysis by Mayhew had been of all incumbents together, and that approach had continued. He found that the percentage of safe seats for incumbents increased abruptly in 1966 and has continued to rise since then.

The results of examining the trend of safe seats by party were clear. From 1946 to 1964 Democrats had far more safe seats than did Republicans: 72.2 percent of Democratic incumbents held safe seats, and 43.6 percent of Republicans were safe. From 1964 to 1966 Republicans experienced a surge in their percentage of safe seats from 21.6 percent to 89.2 percent. Democrats experienced a modest decline, but the decline was not enough to offset the Republican surge, and the overall percentage of safe seats increased from 58.1 percent to 66.1 percent. The percentage for all incumbents remained higher after 1966 because Republicans maintained their new level of safe seats, while Democratic incumbents were less safe. The overall increase was because of changes experienced by Republicans but not all incumbents.

The implication was that an interpretation focusing on changes in the situation of all incumbents might not be the most useful one. Analyses were emerging that indicated that a focus on long-term secular realignments was useful for understanding change (Black and Black, 1987, 2002; Abramowitz and Saunders, 1998; Bartels, 2000; Jacobson, 2003; Stonecash, Brewer, and Mariani, 2003; Polsby, 2004; Stonecash, 2006). If Republicans were the primary beneficiaries of greater incumbency security, then perhaps the focus should be on partisan changes and their effects and not on some general change advantaging all incumbents.

These two encounters with data served as a prompt to take another look at the presumed increase in the incumbency effect. The analysis that follows stems in large part from having stumbled on these puzzling and intriguing findings. The analysis was also prompted by my prior work on secular realignment. It seemed very possible, as will be explained in later chapters, that what appeared to be a greater incumbency effect was really the consequence of secular realignment.[1] It might have looked like a greater incumbency advantage, but changes could be better explained as a result of realignment. The issue became trying to figure out what we would see in electoral patterns if something altogether different (realignment) was driving patterns, rather than an increased incumbency advantage.

This analysis, then, is not a case of presenting a theory and then testing implications. It is first an exploration of whether the trends

---

[1] The focus of this analysis is on *secular* realignment (Key, 1959) and not *critical* realignment. The former focuses on gradual changes in the relative support that parties receive and the movement of some political groups from one party to another. The latter focuses on abrupt changes in overall and group support and has been a prime focus of scholars such as Burnham (1970). As Mayhew (2002) has ably argued, the evidence for the presence of critical realignments as a significant source of change in American politics is weak. Not only is that evidence not strong, but there is also considerable evidence that a secular realignment perspective is far more helpful in explaining changes over the last 50 years (Black and Black, 1987; Jacobson, 2007; Polsby, 2004; Stonecash, 2006).

that are regularly reported are suspect and then an exploration of whether the trends that do exist might be better explained by another perspective.

This issue of whether the incumbency effect has increased is in many ways a dispute about data trends: do they go in the directions presumed? But the implications of the conclusions are much greater. If incumbents are able to use campaign funds and the resources that come with being in office to increase their vote percentages, it suggests that there are reasons to worry about the responsiveness of our politicians and our democracy. It suggests that election results are being altered in ways we should be uneasy about and might try to change. We might limit the resources of office holders and impose greater restrictions on their ability to raise campaign funds. But if the trends have not evolved as suggested, then there are fewer reasons to worry and less reason to be cynical. Indeed, if existing trends are a product of a gradual re-sorting of the relationship between parties and the electorate through realignment, there are reasons to see elections of the last several decades in a very different light. They may not reflect the rejection of partisanship, but rather the re-sorting of partisan attachments and the reassertion of the importance of partisanship.

CHAPTER 2

The Consensus about a Greater Incumbency Effect

In 1974 David Mayhew (1974a) called attention to a significant change in House election results. He classified districts as safe if the incumbent won with 60 percent or more of the vote and marginal if the incumbent received less than that. He then compared the frequency of safe and marginal districts for the years 1946–1972. It was clear that the percentage of marginal districts decreased in 1966. Figure 2.1 shows the percentage of House elections involving incumbents who had marginal outcomes from 1956 to 1972. Something happened in 1966 and in subsequent elections involving incumbents. For 1956–1964 an average of 40.4 percent of House incumbent outcomes were marginal. For 1966–1972 the average was 29.7. Subsequent studies confirmed the existence of this trend (Cover and Mayhew, 1977: 63; Krehbiel and Wright, 1983: 143).

Mayhew's speculative, but very plausible, explanation of this change was that members were allocating themselves more of the resources that could be used to increase their visibility, popularity, and vote percentages. Members were sending out more government-funded mail to constituents, allowing them to boost their visibility. They were performing more constituency services, helping constituents with problems. The number of grant-in-aid programs was increasing, allowing members to claim more credit for bringing benefits to the district. They were doing more for their constituents and had more resources to advertise these efforts (Mayhew, 1974a: 310–11, 1974b: 53–60, 84–85). The combination of these activities was creating more positive visibility for members of Congress, making it harder for challengers to make a dent in their electoral fortunes. Incumbents also had more

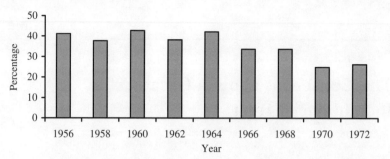

Figure 2.1. Percentage of marginal House seats for incumbents, 1956–1972.

access to polling procedures to monitor the impact of their efforts, making it possible for them to adjust their efforts if problems arose.

There was also other evidence that broad changes were occurring in election results for incumbents. Another important trend is the average percentage of the vote incumbents won over time. Figure 2.2 presents that trend for all contested incumbent races, or those involving a candidate from each major party. The specific data for this figure are presented at the end of Chapter 3. From the 1940s through the late 1980s, incumbents were securing a steadily rising percentage of the vote. Repeated studies confirmed this finding (Born, 1979: 813; Parker, 1980; Alford and Hibbing, 1981: 1051; Garand and Gross, 1984: 21; Gross and Garand, 1984: 227, 234; Jacobson, 1987: 127).

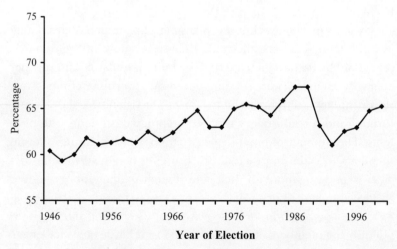

Figure 2.2. Vote percentages for contested incumbents, 1946–2004.

Not only was the overall average vote percentage increasing, but supporting evidence came from studies of initial reelection bids, changes during careers, and what happened when incumbents left office. Members were enhancing the value of incumbency. The *sophomore surge* consists of the ability of incumbents to increase their vote percentages from their initial elections to their first incumbent elections. If the perks of office were becoming more valuable, then there should be an increase in the sophomore surge, and studies indicated that there was (Cover, 1977: 527–28; Cover and Mayhew, 1977: 69–70; Born, 1979: 814–15; Collie, 1981: 124).

Then there is the issue of how vote percentages of incumbents change over the course of their careers. If incumbents were doing better, then their ability to increase their vote with successive years in office should have increased. The evidence indicated they were able to do that (Alford and Hibbing, 1981: 1047–49).

Finally, there should be greater changes after they leave. The *retirement slump* is the loss in partisan support in a district in the election after an incumbent chooses not to run for reelection. If incumbents are able to increase their vote percentages beyond that of the underlying partisan inclination of a district, when an open seat race (no incumbent present) occurs, a new candidate will not have that advantage. The vote percentage for the candidate of the same party as the retiring incumbent should be lower, reflecting the difference in the support an incumbent can create compared to someone just running for the office. If incumbents are becoming more successful in raising their votes, then the difference between the incumbent and the candidate of the same party in an open seat should be increasing over time. Studies found that the retirement slump after 1950 was much higher than for earlier decades (Cover and Mayhew, 1977: 69–70; Payne, 1980: 469–472).

Finally, in an effort to rigorously assess how the incumbency advantage had changed over the last 100 years, Gelman and King (1990) estimated the advantage incumbents had over challengers, after taking into account the prior partisan vote in the district and national partisan swings away or toward the parties over time. Figure 2.3 presents the results for 1900–2000 using their approach. For the first 50 years, incumbents had little advantage. Beginning in the 1950s and 1960s,

Figure 2.3. Estimates of the incumbency advantage, 1904–2000, using the Gelman-King method.

their advantage began to increase and is now considerably higher than it was from 1900 to 1950.

In short, there was a considerable volume of consistent information that the electoral fortunes of incumbents were changing. They are staying in office longer (Polsby, 1968, 2004), and over time, their electoral fortunes were improving. It has become more and more common to refer to the increased incumbency effect as a given of contemporary electoral politics. The focus is primarily on how to explain the advantage of incumbents (Zaller, 1992: 19, 216–64). The effect is found in national elections and in state legislatures (Jewell and Breaux, 1988; Breaux, 1990; Garand, 1991; Cox and Morgenstern, 1993). The conclusion that incumbents have an advantage in the electoral process, and have *increased* that advantage, seems unassailable.

THE POLITICAL CONTEXT

This focus on what was happening to incumbents occurred at a time when changes in American politics and electoral behavior were seen as conducive to a growing incumbency effect. Voters were living in a political context in which the differences between parties were declining. Figure 2.4 shows the average voting records of Democrats and Republicans in the House. Poole and Rosenthal (1984, 1985, 1991, 1997) examined the voting records of all members of the House and created

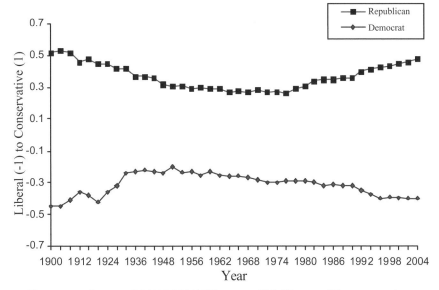

Figure 2.4. Average DW-NOMINATE scores, U.S. House of Representatives, by party, 1952–2004. Data from Keith Poole (http://voteview.com/dwnl. htm).

measures (called a DW-NOMINATE score) of how conservative or liberal their voting records were. According to their analysis, a positive score means that members had conservative voting records, while a negative score means they had liberal voting records. The scores for all Democratic members are averaged, as are those for Republicans. Figure 2.4 shows the average by party and how far apart the averages were for each year. From 1900 through the 1950s the differences had steadily declined, and by the 1960s, there was a time of sustained diminished differences between the parties.

With differences between the parties declining, it would not be surprising to find that voters would be less likely to be attached to parties and less likely to base their vote for a House member on partisan allegiances. The evidence indicates that both of these trends were occurring. At the individual level, National Election Studies surveys found that identification with parties was declining (Converse, 1976: 32, 70), that partisan voting (someone identifying with a party and voting for candidates of that party) was declining, and split-ticket voting was increasing (Nie, Verba, and Petrocik, 1976; Flanigan and Zingale,

1979: 45–60).[1] Aggregate level analyses indicated similar changes. In the decades prior to the 1960s, there was a steady rise in ticket splitting (Burnham, 1965: 13–20). The partisan votes in House districts for House and presidential candidates of the same party, which were once very similar, were steadily diverging (Jones, 1964: 465; Cummings, 1966: 31–39; Burnham, 1975: 428). Partisan presidential and House results within House districts were becoming less connected.

The finding that the electorate was less attached to parties provided an explanation of why incumbents could pull more voters to them. If voters were less attached to parties and less inclined to "vote party" (just voting for the party with which they identified), then they might become more inclined to vote on the basis of relatively greater awareness of incumbents or because incumbents had developed a positive personal identity among voters. An electorate less tied to parties could be moved by various activities to vote for the person. Incumbents could develop support based on a so-called personal vote and achieve a higher percentage of the vote than if voters acted primarily on their partisanship. The activities of incumbents became important to understand, and their activities quickly became central to attempts to explain election results (Wattenberg, 1991; Menefee-Libey, 2000; Brady, Cogan, and Fiorina, 2000: 5; Jacobson, 2001: 24–25; Carson, Engstrom, and Roberts, 2007).[2]

---

[1] There was also a developing interest in how much incumbency (Erikson, 1971) and redistricting (Erikson, 1972; Tufte, 1973) helped the vote percentages of House members.

[2] The central issue was whether change was a result of shifts in electoral behavior, which incumbents had limited control over, or in the activities of incumbents, which they could control (Krehbiel and Wright, 1983: 141). Those who focused on change in the electorate relied heavily on Burnham's (1970, 1975) thesis of electorate disengagement from parties. Using his arguments as a guide, there were efforts to understand whether partisan defection was increasing and how much incumbents had been able to raise their name recognition (Abramowitz, 1975; Cover, 1977: 531–36; Ferejohn, 1977: 169; Mann, 1978; Nelson, 1978–1979; Campbell, 1983; Krehbiel and Wright, 1983). Others focused more on matters incumbents could specifically control. They examined the effects of redistricting (Tufte, 1973; Ferejohn, 1977: 167–68; Ansolabehere, Snyder, and Stewart, 2000), legislator activities and interaction with constituents through mail and casework (Johannes, 1979; Fiorina, 1981; Johannes and McAdams, 1981; Yiannakis, 1981; McAdams and Johannes, 1988, and references therein; Serra and Cover, 1992; Serra, 1994, and references therein; Jacobson, 2001: 21–100), how challengers and their quality matter (Krasno and Green, 1988; Cox and Katz, 1996; Levitt and Wolfram, 1997), and the impact of campaign spending on electoral margins (Jacobson, 1978, 1985, 1990; Abramowitz, 1989, 1991: 48–52).

RECONSIDERING THE EVIDENCE

The accumulated evidence seems fairly clear and consistent that there has been an increase in the electoral fortunes of incumbents, and there is a plausible explanation for the trends found. As sometimes happens with accepted conclusions, however, it is valuable to take another look at the evidence. There are essentially two matters worth examining. First, is the evidence as clear as it may seem? That is, are the data, the analyses of them, and the results supportive of the conclusions reached? Second, might there be another, more plausible explanation of whatever trends do exist?

The next three chapters assess the issue of the evidence for an increased incumbency effect. There are three indicators to be examined to see if the situation of incumbents has improved. These indicators are the average vote received by incumbents, the ability of incumbents to increase their vote percentages over the course of their careers, and the decline in the partisan vote in a district after an incumbent leaves. Together, these three indicators provide a comprehensive portrait of whether incumbents are better off. They capture the situation in any given year, the dynamics of what happens over a career, and the contrast between the presence of an incumbent and his or her absence.

CHAPTER 3

The Trend in Incumbent Vote Percentages

One of the central pieces of evidence of an increased incumbency effect has been the increase in the vote percentage won by incumbents since 1946. Assuming that election results are recorded correctly,[1] the important issue is whether an upward trend actually occurred. As

---

[1] The matter of the accuracy of election results is not discussed in studies, and may not be relevant here. To the extent that analyses are based on Inter-University Consortium for Political and Social Research (ICPSR) study 7757, however, accuracy issues are very important. I began with the data from this ICPSR study and compared it to the election results printed in the *Congressional Quarterly's Guide to U.S. Elections*, volume 2, 4th edition (Congressional Quarterly, 2001) and discovered numerous errors. I then consulted the *Congressional Quarterly's Guide* to try to determine what the results were for a particular district. While the *Congressional Quarterly's Guide* is very valuable, there are third-party candidacies that are not reported in that compilation. In some cases, the vote percentages reported appear to constitute less than 100 percent of all votes recorded in that contest. To try to remedy that problem, I consulted Michael J. Dubin's (1998) *United States Congressional Elections, 1788–1997* to find further results.

Assuming this source is accurate, which I cannot verify, several types of errors were detected and corrected. In some cases the percentage for the Democrat or Republican candidate was missing. In other cases a single-digit percentage was recorded for a Democrat or Republican, but that candidate actually received no votes. One kind of so-called error is particularly noteworthy. In both California and New York, cross-endorsement of candidates has occurred, and still exists in New York. In California a candidate might run with the endorsement of the Democratic and Republican parties. In these cases Dubin (1998) records the party endorsements (lines) of a candidate. I was able to verify the actual party affiliations (not endorsements) of candidates by checking their affiliations in the prior Congress, using either results for prior elections or by consulting the Biographical Directory of the United States Congress (http://bioguide.congress.gov/biosearch/biosearch.asp). In the ICPSR data set, many of these districts have no recorded votes, and these districts end up missing in analyses of vote percentages. In New York, candidates can be cross-endorsed and then have their names listed on both lines. I checked these cases against the official results printed in the *Legislative Manual* for various years.

noted before, Mayhew's (1974a) analysis prompted a focus on this indicator. He made four decisions in creating his trend analysis. First, he began the examination with a focus on incumbent vote percentages. Second, he calculated the percentage of the vote received as a

While the votes on the separate lines should be added together and recorded as only a Democratic or Republican vote, the ICPSR data set records the vote on the Democratic line as the vote for a Democratic candidate and the vote on the Republican line as the vote for a Republican candidate. The result is that a district is recorded as contested and competitive to some degree, when it was uncontested by a major party candidate. Races were recorded as closer than they were. In both of these states I corrected the data. In California I used Dubin (1998) or the Biographical Directory designation of the candidate's actual party affiliation and recorded the total votes for the candidate on that party line. The other party line was given a zero. The logic of this is that the general concern is the partisan vote for major party candidates. In each district, almost all candidates will have an initial party affiliation, and that will be known in the district. If the candidate receives the endorsement of another party, the actual vote is still for a candidate of a specific party. In New York the same logic applies. While a name is listed on two (or more) lines, the party affiliation of each candidate is well known, and the vote is for that candidate, regardless of on which line it is received.

A similar issue involves Minnesota voting. For years the Democrat-Farmer-Labor (DFL) Party served as the vehicle for representing the Democratic Party in the state. The ICPSR shows no vote for Democratic candidates in the years that the DFL was relevant. I recorded the DFL percentages as the Democratic vote. Again, the concern is not the vote percentage recorded on a party line, but the vote percentage that a candidate of a particular party received. The DFL, which operated as a fusion party, should not have no recorded vote because it is a merger of other concerns. Results in Louisiana present a particularly difficult issue of how to record results. For some years Louisiana held an open primary, in which all party candidates could enter. If no candidate received a majority, a runoff would be held between the two candidates with the highest percentages, even if they were in the same party. If a candidate did receive a majority, the individual would appear on the ballot on the traditional Tuesday in November without any apparent opposition. There would then be no recorded votes, making it difficult to record a result. If a candidate received enough votes to avoid a runoff, the apparent result in November was 0 (no votes) or 100 percent for no opponent. Neither option reflected the vote proportion the candidate won in the open primary. In a study of vote percentages of members of Congress, the options of 0 or 100 percent are not satisfactory indicators of the situation the candidate faced.

These races might simply be excluded, but that also is not very satisfactory. An option is to return to the results from Dubin (1998), which presents both the open primary and runoff results. In many of these districts, several Democrats ran along with several Republicans, and the winning percentage might be, for example, only 30 percent, compared to 13 percent for a Republican. Since, in this particular study, the concern is the vote proportion of candidates, and their relative security, the decision in this case is to record the percentages of the leading Democrat and the leading Republican. This is not completely satisfactory since the leading Democrat might receive 30 percent, followed by a Democrat with 22 percent, and then a Republican percentage of the total major party vote. Third, he presented results in terms of the percentage of incumbent outcomes that were safe or marginal. Fourth, he included contested and uncontested races.

Mayhew's (1974a) first two decisions were quickly accepted for subsequent studies. Almost all the studies conducted since his analysis have focused on incumbents and their vote as a percentage of the major party vote. His latter two decisions, however, were set aside, and that has had significant consequences. Rather than use the percentage of marginal or safe seats, Born (1979) argued that with the presentation of outcomes by categories, small percentage changes could result in a shift of many cases between categories and the impression

with 14 percent. Recording only the leading Democrat and Republican will underrepresent the closeness of the second highest vote recipient. That is, however, also a potential issue in a state like California, where the second highest vote recipient could run on the Progressive Party and not show up if only Democrats or Republicans are recorded. While this is a problem, it is minor because the focus in these vote records is on the proportion of winners, and the practice of recording 30 and 14 percent will reflect the percentage of the winner. The virtue of recording these percentages is that the winner actually received only 30 percent, which is not a secure position. Accurately recording and reflecting that low percentage seems appropriate in this case, and is what was done. If a candidate was unopposed in the open primary, the candidate was recorded as unopposed and as receiving 100 percent.

The problems in California and Wisconsin may not have affected results for members of Congress if those doing data runs took care to record the vote of winners, regardless of the party lines involved. If, on the other hand, a district was recorded as having a Democratic or Republican winner, but no percentages were recorded on the Democratic or Republican lines, then these districts might show up as missing in analyses. It is not possible to tell if this occurred because most studies contain no discussions of these specifics. In New York the problem could create clear errors of percentages. If a cross-endorsed Democrat in New York City has his or her vote across two lines, the candidate's vote proportion might be interpreted as 65 percent, when the actual percentage is 95 percent, and there is no major opponent. If only contested races are assessed, the New York situation will lead to this district being included, when it should have been excluded. Again, it is unknown whether this problem actually occurred in published studies because there is no discussion of such issues.

Finally, several decisions about the presence of an incumbent are important. If an incumbent loses the primary in his or her own party, but is still present in the November election on another line, an incumbent is recorded as present. If an incumbent switches parties, but still runs, an incumbent is recorded as present. If two incumbents run against each other, an incumbent is not recorded as present. In this case it is not possible to specify an incumbent percentage versus a challenger percentage, so no incumbent percentage is calculated. If a person was in office, and was elected in a special election within the last two years, even if only weeks or months prior to the general election, he or she is coded as an incumbent.

of a large change. He used the average vote percentage for incumbents (Born, 1979: 812–13), and almost all subsequent efforts to track the trend focused on average vote percentages or changes in them (Payne, 1980: 471–72; Alford and Hibbing, 1981: 1047–51; Garand and Gross, 1984: 21; Gross and Garand, 1984: 230; Jacobson, 1987: 127; Ansolabehere, Snyder, and Stewart, 2000: 24; Jacobson, 2001: 24–26).

The most important decision involved the last decision Mayhew made, or the issue of which races to include. Rather than follow his decision to use all races, the decision was to exclude certain elections, usually without any explanation. Born (1979: 811–12) chose to exclude all multimember, at-large, and uncontested districts. Payne (1980: 469) excluded multicandidate and at-large races and all those in which a winner received more than 89 percent of the vote. The South was excluded by Alford and Hibbing (1981: 1045–46) and Gross and Garand (1984: 226) because of its unique electoral history. Jacobson (1987: 126–27; 2001: 24–26) chose to focus on incumbents with major party opposition.

Surprisingly, these initial decisions about which districts to include received no critical scrutiny. Those researchers who did the first studies largely asserted their sense of what cases were appropriate to include, and others largely replicated this approach to deriving average vote percentages with little questioning. There is almost no evidence of dissent between the two decisions of how to calculate a percentage or which cases to include. Each of these decisions, however, deserves consideration, and each affects the derived trend in vote percentages.

DECISIONS AND THEIR CONSEQUENCES

Each of Mayhew's (1974a) initial decisions and subsequent practices need to be considered for their implications. First is how an electoral outcome should be classified, as marginal or safe or by the vote percentage. Born (1979) argued that the focus should be on average percentages received by incumbents and not just on whether an outcome is or is not marginal. Small shifts in the average could create large shifts in distributions with five percentage point groupings. That point is persuasive, though both can easily be used.

If percentages are used, the next decision involves whether to calculate vote percentages as a percentage of the two-party vote. This
decision is less plausible. In many districts, third-party candidates run
in the November elections. If their votes are excluded from the denom-
inator, it reduces the vote total and increases the apparent vote percentage of incumbents. As an example, assume a Republican wins
53 percent, a Democrat wins 40 percent, and all other candidates
win 7 percent of the total vote. If the third-party vote is excluded,
the Republican winning percentage is now 53/93, or 57.0 percent.
An incumbent would hardly regard a percentage of 53 as secure,
and representing the winning percentage as 57.0 is misleading. More
important, the effect of relying on the percentage of the two-party vote
is to systematically inflate the reported percentages of winning incumbents. If our concern is to track the percentage of the vote received
by incumbents, it seems odd to measure and present percentages that
are not the actual percentages that candidates attain. In the analysis
presented here the actual percentage of the vote (based on all votes
cast for candidates) is used, not the percentage of the two-party vote
received.

A third issue is whether to examine the vote percentages of just
incumbents or of all winners. If the concern is whether incumbents
are able to use their advantage in political resources to increase their
vote percentages, a focus on the former is appropriate. The analytic
difficulty, however, is that if the concern is whether incumbents have
some ability to affect vote percentages that nonincumbents lack, then
trends for both groups need to be examined (Collie, 1981; Garand
and Gross, 1984: 26–27; Gross and Garand, 1984: 232). If an increase
in vote percentages occurs in situations with and without incumbents
present, as Gross and Garand (1984) found, it is questionable logic to
examine just incumbents and then conclude that there is a connection
between incumbent political resources and changes in vote percentages. Nonetheless, since the focus has been only on incumbents, that
practice will be followed here.

The last decision, which elections to include, is perhaps the most
important one. The decision to exclude uncontested districts creates
two serious problems of analysis. First, if the number of districts
excluded varies over time, then the average vote percentage involves a

varying number of districts over time. Second, the number of uncontested districts has a distinct trend over time. The decision to exclude the uncontested races as not meaningful has a significant impact on the resulting trend in the vote percentages for incumbents and winners in the House. *This decision is in large part the source of the trend that has received so much attention.*

The essential issue is the effect of including or adding in previously uncontested districts. A district that changes from being uncontested to contested rarely immediately produces a competitive district. When uncontested races are excluded, but then included when the district changes to being contested, it invariably involves adding to the average a district with a relatively high vote percentage for the incumbent. The addition of the previously uncontested race, with its higher than average vote percentage, contributes to the impression that the average winning percentage is increasing. If there is a steady decline across several consecutive years in the number of uncontested races, this means that each year districts not previously included are added to the average. These "new" districts were contested and in the first year they are contested they have *relatively* high vote percentages for the incumbent. The result of successively adding in these districts is the impression of a rising average percentage, when the real source of change is the addition of previously uncontested districts.

Table 3.1 presents some examples of how such transitions in vote percentages within districts occur. The examples involve selected Mississippi districts from 1954 to 1972, a time of partisan change in the South. In 1954, all the House districts in the table voted 100 percent Democratic and were excluded from the analysis. During the 1960s Republicans began to contest elections in these districts. The emergence of Republican candidates added these districts to the analysis of contested elections. With one exception (district 4 in 1964), the percentage added by these districts to the analysis was higher than the national average of approximately 61 percent, which prevailed for other contested seats. The addition of these newly contested cases would raise the national average.

The issue, then, is whether the number of uncontested races has been increasing or declining over time, such that deleting or

TABLE 3.1. *Democratic and incumbent percentages in selected Mississippi House districts, 1954–1972*

| | House district | | | | | | | | |
| | 1 | | 2 | | 4 | | 6 | | 7 | |
Year	Dem.	Inc.	Dem.	Inc.	Dem.	Inc.	Dem.	Inc.	Dem.	Inc.
1954	100	100	100	100	100	100	100	100	100	100
1956	100	100	100	100	100	100	100	100	100	100
1958	100	100	100	100	100	100	100	100	100	100
1960	94	94	100	100	100	100	100	100	86	86
1962	100	100	100	100	83	83	100	100	70	70
1964	100	100	100	100	44	56	100	100	63	63
1966	69	69	84	84			70	70	77	77
1968	100	100	100	100	70	70	100	100	80	80
1970	100	100	87	87	100	100	90	90	100	100
1972	100	100	62	62					100	100

An empty cell means the seat was open, or no incumbent was present. Abbreviations are as follows: Dem., percentage received by the Democratic incumbent; Inc., percentage received by the incumbent.

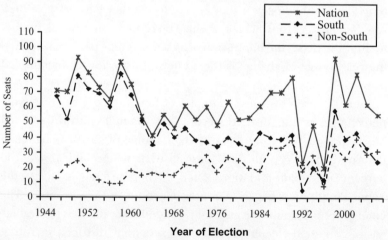

Figure 3.1. Number of incumbents uncontested, for the nation and by region, 1946–2006.

adding cases might affect the average. Figure 3.1 indicates the number of uncontested races per year since 1946.[2] Most, but not all,

---

[2] The table presents the specific data for each year on: the number of uncontested races for incumbents running for reelection and for all districts; the number of

of these uncontested elections during the 1950s and 1960s were in the South. If the focus is on contested races for incumbents or all

contested races for all incumbents and for all districts; and the average vote won for each of these categories.

Data on house elections, 1946–2006: incumbent average percentage of vote won and number contested and uncontested

Year	All		Contested	
	No.	Average %	No.	Average %
1946	381	68.3	310	61.5
1948	388	67.6	320	61.2
1950	400	69.4	307	60.6
1952	373	70.5	290	62.3
1954	400	68.3	327	61.4
1956	403	67.7	338	61.5
1958	391	70.5	300	62.0
1960	402	68.6	327	61.6
1962	382	67.4	328	62.5
1964	393	65.9	352	62.1
1966	404	67.7	349	63.0
1968	401	67.0	355	63.1
1970	395	69.5	334	64.5
1972	376	68.4	324	63.9
1974	382	68.9	322	63.6
1976	381	69.1	333	65.2
1978	377	71.0	313	65.6
1980	391	69.6	339	65.3
1982	371	68.8	317	64.6
1984	407	70.8	344	66.0
1986	396	73.1	326	67.9
1988	409	73.3	339	68.2
1990	404	68.9	324	63.0
1992	346	64.0	323	62.1
1994	389	66.9	341	62.9
1996	381	65.2	361	63.4
1998	403	71.2	310	65.0
2000	417	69.1	354	65.5
2002	386	71.5	305	66.4
2004	408	69.9	348	65.7
2006	403	67.2	348	63.5
Averages				
1946–1964		68.4		61.7
1966–2006		69.1		64.7
1956–1964		68.0		61.9
1966–1972		68.2		63.6

Source: Compiled from Dubin (1998) and records of the House of Representatives.

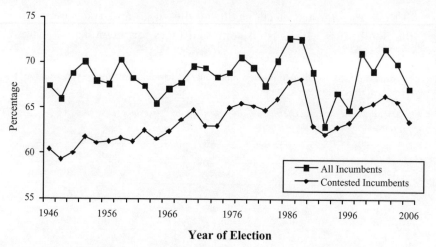

Figure 3.2. Vote percentages for contested incumbents and all incumbents, 1946–2006.

winners,[3] beginning in the late 1950s, there was a steady addition to the calculation of the average vote percentage of district outcomes with relatively high vote percentages.

While there are reasons to think that the exclusion and then addition of uncontested races matters, does it actually affect the reported trend? And if it does make a difference, should we include or exclude uncontested contests? Figure 3.2 provides the trend lines for the average vote percentages (actual, not of the two-party vote) received for contested races and for all incumbents. The bottom trend line represents the average vote percentage of contested incumbents. Winning and losing incumbents are included in both trends. The top line represents the average for all incumbents who ran. The bottom line shows the much discussed rising trend, and particularly for the years up to 1990. The top line shows a very different pattern. The percentages are relatively flat and within the range of 65–70 percent, except for the

---

[3] Given the predominance of these races in the South, a plausible solution is to exclude the South, as some have done (Gross and Garand, 1984). The difficulty with this decision is that the South has steadily become more competitive, and excluding the South means excluding many contested districts. At some point this must stop, creating a significant disjuncture in a time series. If the trend is the object of analysis, this approach is unsatisfactory.

TABLE 3.2. *Trend patterns: contested incumbents and all incumbents, 1946–2006*

	N	b	r^2	Probability
Contested				
1946–2006	31	.08	.44	.00
1956–1972	9	.23	.82	.00
All				
1946–2006	31	.02	.01	.40
1956–1972	9	.03	.01	.78

relatively large fluctuations that occur around 1990. It appears that which races are included has a significant impact on the trend.

To provide a more precise description of the two trends, Table 3.2 presents the regression of these averages on the year of the election to capture the time trend. If there is an upward trend in the percentages of incumbents, then the relationship between the average percentage and time (the slope) should be positive. These results indicate that the choice of contested and uncontested elections matters a great deal. If only contested incumbents are examined over the time period 1946–2006, there is a clear positive trend in averages, and year (for time trend) explains a considerable proportion of the variance. If the time span is confined to the years Mayhew (1974a) examined, 1956–1972, the upward trend is even more pronounced. The trend for all incumbents is very different. For both time periods, there is essentially no trend, and time explains no variance. It is clear that it matters which contests are examined. The research of the last 30 years about rising incumbency vote percentages has focused on a trend that is a result of deciding to exclude uncontested districts.

The fundamental issue, then, is whether only contested or all elections should be examined. There are several reasons why excluding uncontested races is a very questionable decision. First, if the concern is tracking closeness of incumbent electoral outcomes over time, then excluding uncontested races misrepresents the average percentage of the vote received by incumbents. Given that in some years, there were more than 80 uncontested elections involving incumbents, almost one-fourth of House elections involving incumbents are excluded.

Second, the decision excludes districts where the parties are particularly strong, thus treating districts that lean heavily to one party as not
relevant. It is an odd rule to purport to assess the strength of incumbents, while excluding those who do particularly well. Furthermore,
if the spatial distribution of partisan populations shifts over time such
that like-minded partisan populations cluster together and become
spatially segregated from each other, there will be more districts that
heavily favor one party, and these districts might end up excluded
from calculations. Even if the district does not change, and an incumbent has intimidated challengers from entering the race, these are the
very cases that should be included because they represent examples
of very successful incumbents. If the goal is to measure the ability of
incumbents to improve their situations, it seems strange to remove
those who achieved the ultimate goal of no opponent. Third, it is
even more questionable to set up the calculation of an average that
in one year excludes a district with no opponent, and then, after an
opponent appears in the next year, includes the district. The result
is to add during the next year an incumbent with a relatively high
percentage, which raises the average. In sum, the contested average
embodies three questionable rules. It does not include all incumbent
outcomes. In excluding uncontested races, it excludes cases where
incumbents do particularly well. It also sets up a rule that, with a
downward trend in uncontested races, results in a rising average that
is a product of the rule and not a reflection of the reality of election
outcomes.

Finally, we should be skeptical of relying on a rule that results in the
appearance of less competitive elections at the very time uncontested
elections were declining on the national scene. From 1950 to 1964
the number of uncontested incumbent races fell from 93 to 41. After
decades of a situation in which region was a defining feature of party
bases, competition between the parties was becoming more national in
scope. Both parties were mutually contesting more districts nationally.
Yet the decision rule of excluding uncontested races from calculations
led to the conclusion that competition was declining.

In short, one of the central bits of evidence for the argument that
incumbents were doing well is suspect. Instead, the evidence indicates that more races were being contested and the average of all

incumbents was essentially flat, with some erratic fluctuations from time to time. This first major indicator of a growing incumbency effect is thus questionable.

QUANTITATIVE ESTIMATIONS OF THE INCUMBENCY EFFECT

The evidence to support the argument that incumbents are now doing better than in prior decades is weak. This evidence, direct as it is, might be seen as too simple. One effort to conduct a more rigorous analysis was developed by Gelman and King (1990). They were troubled by biased estimates in prior work and employed multiple regression to derive an unbiased estimate of the incumbency advantage over time. Their analysis indicated a significant and sustained increase in the incumbency effect in 1966. It is an analysis that has become accepted (Cox and Katz, 1996), elaborated on (Gelman and Huang, forthcoming), and used to summarize the post–World War II trend in the incumbency effect (Brady, D'Onofrio, and Fiorina, 2000: 136; Jacobson, 2004: 26–27).

Given Gelman and King's (1990) conclusion, some commentary on their analysis is necessary. Their approach, while seemingly logical and plausible, has some serious limitations. While dissecting their analysis is technical in nature, it is important to do so because their approach is cited as having generated a definitive assessment of the incumbency advantage. Appendix A presents a detailed critique of their approach and is presented for readers with some background in multiple regression. Only a summary will be presented here.

Gelman and King's (1990) approach is to predict the vote in a district based on past outcomes and then estimate how much an incumbent's vote differs from that predicted percentage. If that incumbent difference grows over time, then the incumbency advantage is increasing. Specifically, they estimate the vote percentage for a current election (say, 1966) from the vote from the prior election (1964), determine who won the prior election (in 1964), and then add a variable for the presence or absence of an incumbent (in 1966). The problem with their approach is that the high correlation among all these conditions produces an unanticipated outcome. The problem is not a bias issue; rather, the problem is that the analysis tracks something other than that which it purports to track.

The variables in Gelman and King's (1990) analysis all capture essentially the same partisan degree of support in a district, leading to high associations among the variables. There is high multicollinearity. When variables have this degree of association and an incumbent is present, regressing the current vote on the prior vote percentage and on who won the seat before leaves little variation to explain in the current vote; that is, 1966 results are predicted so well by 1964 results, *when an incumbent is present,* that there is little left to explain by the presence of a Democratic or Republican incumbent score.

The most important, and most technical, matter is that controlling means that the incumbency variable is also regressed on the prior outcome variables (see Appendix B). This process also leaves little variation in this variable.

The only significant remaining variation occurs in cases of open seats, and it is this that creates their results. When an incumbent chooses not to run (in 1966), the incumbent variable has a score of zero. This recorded score (no incumbent) is a significant deviation from that expected. If a Democrat won in 1964 and had a high percentage of the vote, a Democratic incumbent is (statistically) expected in 1966. If the incumbent vacates the seat, a divergence from the expected is created. This divergence (deviation) is then correlated with whatever change occurs in the partisan vote in these open seats from 1964 to 1966. While Gelman and King's (1990) approach is intended to pick up voting patterns for incumbents, it ends up picking up the association between these unexpected open seat deviations and how much the partisan vote changes from year to year when an open seat occurs.

Gelman and King's (1990) technique finds a significant change in the incumbency effect in the 1960s, but what really changed in the 1960s was the partisan vote from year to year when open seats occurred (see Appendix B). From 1900 through the 1950s, there was little change in the partisan vote from one election to the next when an open seat occurred; that is, when an incumbent retired, the vote did not change much. Beginning in the 1960s, the partisan vote from one open seat to another began to change significantly, and that pattern persisted in subsequent years. Gelman and King's technique picks up the changes occurring in open seats beginning in the 1960s and not the ability of incumbents to separate their votes from some average or prior set of conditions.

Gelman and King's (1990) analysis is a case where the logic of the analysis may be plausible, but the application of the technique generates results different from what is intended. Again, a reader interested in the details of that conclusion should review Appendix B. The important matter is that the results generated by this approach involve another case in which the evidence for an increased incumbency effect does not hold up to scrutiny.

CHAPTER 4

Cumulative Career Changes

There has been no increase in the average incumbent vote percentage since the 1940s. While this evidence is interesting, it has one significant limitation. It is essentially a static analysis – analyzing all incumbents at one point in time – and represents the average vote percentage for any given year. It does not capture the changes experienced by incumbents during their careers. Some incumbents are in their fourth year in office, and others may be in their twentieth.

The yearly average could be very misleading about what happens to incumbents over the course of their careers. A stable average vote percentage for incumbents from year to year may conceal considerable change in career progressions. Over time, incumbents could begin with lower initial percentages but increase their vote percentages at faster rates. The cycle of retirements and new entrants could somehow combine to produce a stable average over time, while the ability of incumbents to increase their vote percentages during their careers is increasing.

To track the dynamics of incumbent electoral fortunes, this chapter examines career changes for House members. The focus is on their ability to increase their vote percentages with successive years in office and the net increase in their vote percentages from the beginning to the end of their careers.

THE POPULATION OF INCUMBENTS

Before analyzing these two indicators of incumbent fortunes, it is helpful to review just how many incumbents there have been since

TABLE 4.1. *Distribution of careers for House members, 1900–2006*

No. of careers	No. of members	Percentage
1	3,538	95.5
2	154	4.2
3	13	.4
TOTAL	3,885	100.0

The total number of 3,885 careers is derived as follows. There are 3,538 members with one career plus 154 with two careers, for another 308, plus another 13 with three careers, for another 39. The total is 3,885 separate careers.
Source: Data compiled by the author.

1900 in the House and how they have left. A legislative career is often discussed as if it constitutes one continuous string of years in office.[1] The difficulty is that there are a considerable number of cases in which a member left because of defeat or voluntary exit and then returned. Some even returned a third time. Table 4.1 indicates the distribution of careers for all members elected in 1900 and after who have left the

[1] It is important to note a difference of this analysis from a previous one. As noted in Footnote 2 of this chapter, I began this analysis by drawing on the work that John Hibbing (1991) did on congressional careers. In the course of reviewing and updating his data set, I became aware that cases of interrupted careers were treated to some extent in that data set as continuous careers. If someone served from 1950 to 1954 and then from 1960 to 1966, Hibbing's data set generally coded this person as having a career running from 1950 to 1966. For my analysis I created a separate case for each year a member served and coded each case with the year of election and the last year served for that string of continuous years of service. If a member served for the years listed previously, then there are two separate careers involved. They are recorded as follows:

Year of election	Initial year	Last year	Length of service (years)
1950	1950	1954	4
1952	1950	1954	4
1960	1960	1966	6
1962	1960	1966	6
1964	1960	1966	6

In Hibbing's (1991, Chap. 2) analysis of careers, there is no mention of interrupted careers and how they were handled. He may have excluded cases of interruption, and he may have included them and there were just missing data for cases when someone was out of office. Since how these cases were handled is not known, the results he presents in his Chapter 2 may or may not be comparable to the ones presented in this analysis.

House. Since the concern is complete careers, those members who have been elected after 1900 but who are still in the House as of 2007 are excluded from this analysis. Their vote percentages may increase or decrease before they leave, and there is no way to know how their careers will end.[2] Of the 3,705 members in the House during those years, 95.5 percent had one continuous career. One hundred fifty-four members left and then returned for another career.[3] Another 13 had three separate spans of service in the House. For this analysis, each continuous span of service is treated as a separate career. This creates a total of 3,885 careers.

How did these incumbents depart the House? The popular impression is that incumbents rarely lose, and almost all academic commentary supports that view.[4] Despite that seeming consensus, many incumbents end their careers with a loss. Of the 3,885 careers since 1900, 2,318 left voluntarily (retired) and 1,567 lost their last elections. Overall, a voluntary exit occurred for 59.7 percent, and 40.3 percent left via defeat. Figure 4.1 indicates the percentage of exits via loss or voluntary retirement over time.[5] This understates incumbent losses because it excludes the roughly 10 percent who lost in a primary.[6]

[2]   It is possible, of course, that relatively recent incumbents represent a new cohort that will be much more successful electorally and may change the results presented here. Only time will tell if that is the case.

[3]   Many of these multiple careers occurred in districts in which the election outcomes were close and two candidates competed with each other regularly. Illinois 21 presents an example of this.

[4]   This so-called fact of American politics is regularly stated: "'It's hard to defeat an incumbent.' This is elementary political wisdom" (Payne, 1980: 465); "One of the most elementary facts of political life in America is incumbent members of the House of Representatives are seldom defeated for reelection" (Campbell, 1983: 434); "House incumbents are among the most electorally secure; most win by large margins, few are defeated in the general election, and very few indeed lose in the primary election" (Aldrich, 1995: 188); "Over the period 1946–2002, only 1.7 percent of officeholders have been defeated in primaries and only 6.1 percent have lost general elections" (Jacobson, 2004: 23).

[5]   There is also the category of death in office or departure because of scandal. These lead to exits between elections. When the data set was created, no coding was made for these types of exits, so no distinction was made for that type of departure. There are often several of these types of exits within an election cycle. Those cases are regarded as voluntary exits for this analysis.

[6]   The issue of how members exit has not received a great deal of attention. One of the few analyses to track the eventual way in which incumbents exited was done by Robert Erikson (1976). He tracked the 435 members elected in 1952 and found

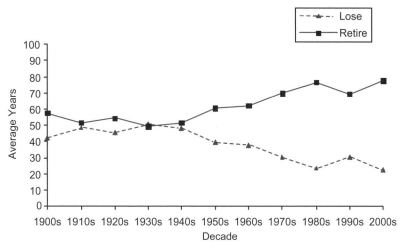

Figure 4.1. Percentages of exits from the House, by type of exit and decade of departure, 1900–2006.

This percentage of exits via a loss does not conform with the general impression that incumbents rarely lose. The discrepancy is because statistics about results in any given year and statistics about final outcomes focus on very different things and are calculated very

that "about one-quarter (25.3 percent) of those gone by 1973 left because they eventually lost in a general election. An additional 10.3 percent eventually lost a primary. *Thus at least one congressman in three eventually is thrown out of office*" (Erikson, 1976: 627). That percentage is very similar to the results for 1900–2006. Perhaps the most interesting finding that Erikson presents is that those members with a more recent entry into the House are more likely to exit via defeat. The rate of exit via defeat by years of entry is as follows: entry 1905–1942, 25.6 percent; 1943–1948, 34.2 percent; 1949–1952, 38.6 percent; 1953, 47 percent (Erikson, 1976: 629). While a consensus was developing that incumbents were safer, his evidence indicated that they were less safe.

Erikson notes that 10.3 percent of members lost via a primary. To provide a check on this, I took all members leaving the House through retirement and checked the biography presented in the Biographical Directory of the United States Congress (http://bioguide.congress.gov/biosearch/biosearch.asp). This biographical information distinguishes between members who failed in their "bid for renomination" and their "bid for reelection." The former refers to cases in which the party did not renominate the incumbent as its candidate. I found that slightly over 10 percent of those incumbents who ran in one year and did not run two years later failed in their bid for renomination. That means that the actual percentage of incumbents who exit via a loss over this time period is probably about 50 percent. This 10 percent error rate has implications for the data analysis presented here. It means that some of the cases used for the retirement slump calculation should be excluded. It also presents problems for trying to track the net change in the vote percentage received differently. An analysis of exits treats an incumbent as one case (ignoring past elections, no matter how many), while most analyses focus on outcomes within one year.

An example may help explain the difference. Assume that the House has 100 members, all elected in some specific year. If 5 percent of that initial class loses in any given year (and they are replaced by incumbents who stay beyond the end of this example), after 10 years (five more elections), then 25 members have left via losses. If the remaining members all retire at the end of 10 years, then 75 incumbents left voluntarily. Over that time period, 95 percent of incumbents routinely won reelection. Yet at the end of 10 years, 25 percent of all initial incumbents left office via a loss. While almost all win within any given year, cumulatively, many may exit via a loss. The point is that when the focus is on careers, incumbents are not as safe as is often stated. Many do leave via a loss.

INITIAL PERCENTAGES

The concern here is with what happens to incumbent vote percentages once someone is in office. There is, however, the issue of whether incumbent starting percentages might have changed over time. If starting percentages have declined considerably, the combination of lower initial percentages but rising vote percentages over a career might explain stable average percentages within a year. Figure 4.2 indicates the average starting percentage of incumbents elected since 1900 who have ended their career in the House. Some minor fluctuation has occurred over time, ranging between 58.7 and 63.8 percent, but there is no trend evident. Percentages were 58.9 percent in the 1900s and 59.1 percent in the 2000–2006 elections. Incumbents are not starting in any more of a safe situation now than in the past.

over a career, which was discussed earlier. For those incumbents losing in a primary, I know of no data source that lists the percentages received in primary elections. Without that data it is not possible to record a percentage for the end of a career. That means that the data analysis on net career changes should not be regarded as definitive. The cases in which a primary loss was the source of the exit are not recorded, and the last percentage used is that for the last general election outcome, which is not accurate. If I can find primary outcomes, I will seek to correct that in future analyses.

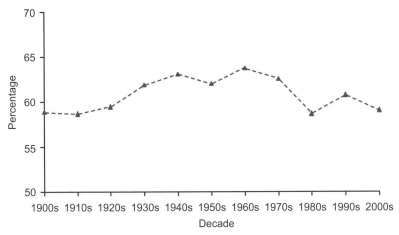

Figure 4.2. Average starting vote percentage for incumbents by decade of departure, 1900–2006. Data compiled by the author.

INCREASING VOTE PERCENTAGES OVER A CAREER

The argument about the growing incumbency advantage is that incumbents can exploit their access to a diverse array of resources to improve their electoral fortunes during their careers and that they are now more successful in these efforts than in the past. There are two problems with accepting this general conclusion. First, while the sense that incumbents improve their electoral fortunes over their careers is widely mentioned, it is rarely actually measured. Second, the implicit historical comparison – the present versus the past – is never conducted, but rather is assumed.

The concept of improving electoral fortunes refers to changes over time in the vote percentage an incumbent receives. On average, from the beginning of their careers to the end, members should be able to steadily increase their vote percentages. Someone who starts with 55 percent in the district should be able to increase it. Furthermore, an incumbent in the years 1946–2006 should be more successful at this than an incumbent serving in the years 1900–1944.

While the general concept refers to change over a career, change over successive elections has been only occasionally assessed (Alford and Hibbing, 1981; Hibbing, 1991: 25–56). The sophomore surge, or the change in vote percentage from the first to the second election, only involves change for one election. A legislator might gain votes, but not be able to further increase his or her vote percentage. The important matter is the general pattern of increases in vote percentages over a career.

To assess the ability of incumbents to increase their vote proportion in successive terms, we need a measure of how an incumbent's vote percentage progresses over time. This can be done by estimating a regression slope of the vote percentages of an incumbent on successive years in office; that is, we estimate how time in office predicts vote percentages. Hibbing (1991) first employed this measure, using the regression of an incumbent's vote percentage on years in office.[7]

The first election that a member serves for any continuous span of service is coded as zero, and subsequent elections are assigned the number of years that an incumbent has been in office. The first reelection is assigned 2 (unless the individual was elected in a special election in the prior year, which would result in a value of 1 for the first reelection bid), and each successive election is assigned an increment of 2.[8]

---

[7] Hibbing (1991) developed a data set of the careers of House members, covering careers up until 1976. I gathered data on elections from then until 2006, including special elections. His data set includes the first year a member was elected, the year a member left, and the number of terms a member served. These career data were merged with House election results, creating a data set in which each case is a single election for a member. If a member serves for 10 terms, that results in 10 cases, with the variable term for each election equal to the number of years a member has served at the time of the election.

   While this analysis builds on Hibbing's (1991) data, the results for earlier eras will not be equivalent because of errors I found in his data set and differences in how some cases were handled. For some members the beginning and ending years are in error. Sometimes this is because special elections or deaths were not incorporated. There are also differences in how some cases are handled. The most important matter involves members who left (either voluntarily or through defeat) and then came back. In Hibbing's data set, many of these cases were coded as having a continuous career. As noted in Footnote 1 I recoded these as three separate careers. Someone who served from 1921 to 1924 and then from 1931 to 1938 was coded as serving two terms for four years and then as four terms for eight years.

[8] If someone ran for office once and won and then chose not to run again, he or she is not included in the analysis. The incumbent's initial percentage is not included and does not affect the intercept. Incumbents were included only if they chose to run at least once for reelection. They were included for all terms they then ran for reelection, even if they lost. In a few cases a House member lost and then came back several years later to run and won again. These cases were treated as new incumbents. I include contested and uncontested elections. The focus here is on all House elections, not some subset of them (see Stonecash, 2003).

The slope is the average increase in the vote percentage as the number of years in office increases. If the slope is positive, it means that every successive election results in a higher vote percentage.

This approach also makes it possible to deal with the issue of how recent decades compare with the past. The analyses that have been done previously present increases for the years since 1946, yet the argument is often about how the present (1946 to now) compares with the past. There are, of course, also many analyses that focus on pre- and post-1965, but the implication of most analyses has been that somehow, the contemporary House is different from the past. Estimating slopes makes it possible to compare the relationship of vote percentage to time in office in one era (however defined) with that in another.

There are several comparisons that are very important. Since the argument is that the post–World War II ability to increase the vote is greater than that ability for earlier years, then the slope for the years 1946–2006 should be greater than the slope for 1900–1944. There is also the more specific argument that something happened in 1966 to increase this ability (slope) to increase vote percentages. If that is the case, then it should be that the slopes for the years 1966–1972 or 1966–2006 should be greater than the slope for 1946–1964. The issue is whether the slopes are more positive in later years, meaning that in elections held in some subset of later years, members of the House can increase their vote percentages with successive years at a greater rate than in prior years.

While an estimation of the bivariate relationship between vote percentages and years in office has a simple appeal, it does not acknowledge that incumbents begin with very different electoral situations. Some begin their careers in districts heavily inclined to elect a Democrat or a Republican, such that their initial vote percentages are relatively high. Others begin in competitive districts with lower percentages. There needs to be recognition of where incumbents start. If one started at 55 and another at 65, the goal is to track the ability to increase a vote percentage from its initial level. With that in mind, each election result (case) used in the analysis has the initial percentage that an incumbent received, along with the vote percentage for successive elections and the number of years someone has served as of

TABLE 4.2. *Effect of years in office, overall and by time groupings, excluding those serving one term and not running for reelection, 1900–2006*

Time period	N	Intercept	Initial %	No. of years	R^2
1900–2006	24,112	22.4	.67	.37	.41
1900–1944	9,736	14.5	.76	.54	.55
1946–2006	14,372	29.8	.57	.28	.29
1946–1964	4,788	20.8	.68	.28	.47
1966–1978	3,236	33.2	.52	.23	.24
1980–2006	5,871	36.6	.48	.28	.17

The *N*s here refer to the number of elections involved. A case is an election year and involves the independent variables of the initial percentage an incumbent received and the year of a legislator's career. The dependent variable is the vote percentage of a legislator in that year. If a legislator serves 10 years, the initial election is coded as zero for the year, and the fifth election is coded as 10 for the number of years in office. The analysis includes all members of the House elected in 1900 or after. Elections are grouped by the years of the election.

that election.[9] The initial vote percentage is used as a control.[10] The regression slope is a measure of the average pattern of change over time between vote percentages and years in office, controlling for the starting percentage of an incumbent.

Table 4.2 presents the results of these analyses. The results are first presented for the years 1900–2006 to provide an overall estimate of the relationship between years in office and the vote percentages of incumbents. Then the comparison of all elections held in 1900–1944

[9] Each record has the unique ICPSR number for each member of the House, his or her initial vote, his or her vote for the current year, and the number of years the member has been in office. Records or cases look like the following:

Year	ICPSR#	Initial vote %	Vote % for current election year	Years
1956	12,221	55.0	55.0	0
1958	12,221	55.0	58.0	2
1960	12,221	55.0	61.0	4
1962	12,222	64.0	64.0	0
1964	12,222	64.0	67.0	2
1966	12,222	64.0	68.0	4

[10] Technically, this means that each slope is estimated for a group of incumbents who started with the same vote percentage. Otherwise, estimations would be conducted as if all incumbents had the same intercept or beginning percentage. Given the enormous variation in starting percentages, if the initial percentage is not included, the resulting R^2s are only about 0.05–0.06.

and elections held in 1946–2006 is presented.[11] For all years, the most significant impact on an incumbent's vote percentage is the initial percentage he or she received[12]; that is, the percentage an incumbent receives in later years is primarily a function of where he or she started. Initial percentages constrain later percentages. The focus here, however, is on how successive years increase the vote percentage. That relationship or slope is positive. Incumbents, on average, after controlling for where they started, are able to increase their vote percentages by .32 with each successive year in office. If an incumbent began with 60 percent of the vote, on average, after 10 years, that incumbent

[11] In this analysis the grouping is done by years of election, for all those incumbents first elected in 1900 and after. This means that some incumbents might be included in both sets of years. This is done because the argument about the incumbency effect has largely been about the changing resources available to incumbents in different eras. While this grouping makes considerable sense, it also makes sense to group incumbents by when they were elected. Fiorina (1977b) has argued that politics is attracting a different type of politician, such that it might also be appropriate to group incumbents by the years of election. While this alternative grouping is worth exploring, it is important to note that this creates a situation in which incumbents elected prior to 1946, and who had lengthy careers that continued into the 1960s and 1970s and perhaps beyond, are assigned to the first grouping. That means that incumbents who might have adapted to increased resources are considered in the first grouping. No grouping is without its problems.

Nonetheless, this alternative grouping is of interest. If this is done, the results are somewhat different. The following table indicates the results if this alternative grouping is used. The initial election percentage has less impact in the latter set of years, while the coefficient for the increase in vote percentages with increasing years in office is essentially the same for the two eras. While these results do not indicate a decline in the effect of the number of years, there is no increase. Regardless of how cases are grouped, there is no evidence of an increase in the ability to increase vote percentages with greater years in the House.

The incumbency effect, overall and by years initially elected

Years elected	N	Intercept	Initial %	# years	R^2
1900–2006	22,398	22.4	.68	.32	.41
1900–1944	10,497	16.0	.76	.31	.54
1946–2006	11,760	30.6	.56	.32	.26

[12] For all the analyses included in the table, the standardized regression coefficient for the initial percentage is three to five times the coefficient for the number of years that an incumbent serves. The initial percentage an incumbent receives has by far the greatest impact on his or her subsequent success. Members who start out in more partisan districts (and with higher initial percentages) retain relatively high percentages.

increased his or her vote percentage by 3.7 percentage points to 63.7 percent. While there is no clear standard by which to judge what is a substantively significant slope, this effect over 10 years seems distinctly modest. A member of Congress who devotes 10 years to representing a district, building visibility, responding to constituents, and bringing home federal benefits, yet realizes, on average, an increase of 3.7 percentage points, has not significantly altered his or her electoral fortune.

While the substantive assessment of the rate of increase in vote percentages with successive years in office (the slope) is ultimately subjective, the comparison of eras can be more precise. When incumbents are grouped by years of elections, the slope of vote percentage on years for 1946–2006 (.28) is less than the slope for 1900–1944 (.54); that is, the ability of incumbents to increase their vote percentages with each year in office is less in the post–World War II era than in the prior 50 years. Incumbents in elections since 1946 are not doing better than before, defined here as the time period of 1900–1944.

This simple grouping of all incumbents together since 1946 might be regarded as inappropriate since Mayhew (1974a) argued that the major change occurred in 1966. To assess that possibility, incumbents are grouped by 1946–1964 and 1966–1978 to compare the years right after World War II with some limited number of years beginning with 1966. The slope coefficient (on years served) for elections held from 1966 to 1978 is .23 and is less than the slope coefficient for 1946–1964, which is .28. The coefficient for 1980–2006 (.28) is the same as for 1946–1966. The R^2 declines for each successive grouping of years, indicating that the ability to explain vote percentages with initial percentage and years in office declines over time.

These results do not indicate that there was an increase in the ability of incumbents to increase their vote percentages with successive years in office for the time period 1946–2004 compared to 1900–1946 or for 1966–1978 compared to 1946–1964. Indeed, it appears that the impact of longer service has steadily declined compared to the first half of the century.[13] Incumbents serving successive years realized less

---

[13] These results indicate that members are not more successful in increasing their vote percentages with successive years in office. This year-to-year relationship must be separated from their ability to create a net increase in their vote percentages over

of a gain in vote percentages in recent decades than they did in the first half of the 1900s.

THE POSSIBILITY OF DECLINING PERCENTAGES OVER A CAREER

The estimations presented thus far are all linear and presume a constant increase in vote percentages with successive years in office. This assumes that an increase from 4 to 6 years produces the same vote change as an increase from 14 to 16 and 24 to 26 years. While this presumption (and imposition) of a linear relationship makes comparing relationships across time very easy, that presumption may be in error, and that error may undermine the validity of the results presented in

a career. The net change is a product of the year-to-year change and the number of years that members stay in office. Over the last century the length of time House members are staying in office has steadily increased (Polsby, 1968, 2004). A member may experience small increases in his or her vote percentage but stay for a lengthy number of years, with the net effect that by the time a career is ended, a member has changed his or her final vote percentage a great deal from his or her initial vote percentage. This would create a greater net change over a career for 1946–2004 compared to 1900–1944.

The following table presents the distribution of net changes in vote percentages for members, from their initial victories to their last races. The distribution is organized by the decade of leaving office. This focuses only on those who have left and excludes those still in the House. Over time the length of careers has increased, as has the net change. Most of the increase in the net change is because of longer careers.

Average net change in members' vote percentages and average years in office by decade left office

| Entering decade | N | Averages | |
		Length	Net Change
1900–1909	231	4.5	−4.5
1910–1919	464	6.0	−3.1
1920–1929	395	7.2	−.3
1930–1939	511	8.3	−3.2
1940–1949	473	7.9	−3.0
1950–1959	326	9.9	−.8
1960–1969	332	11.9	−1.2
1970–1979	380	13.4	1.9
1980–1989	258	11.1	6.6
1990–1999	361	13.3	1.7
2000–2006	152	13.4	8.3

Table 4.2. The problem could be as follows. Members who stay for lengthy careers may tire of the job and pay less attention to the district and eventually suffer erosion in their district support. Or the district may change. Regardless, their support may decline, and that could lead to a curvilinear relationship between years in office and levels of support. Voting support first increases, peaks, and then declines. This possibility is particularly important for comparing eras because members in the 1946–2006 era are staying longer than did members in the 1900–1944 era. If many members in the latter era stay to the point that their support erodes, then the relationship between years and voting support in the latter era is being dragged down by this erosion of support in the later stages of their careers. In other words, in the earlier era, there are fewer cases of long service and declining support. When a linear regression coefficient is fit in the earlier era, there are far fewer cases of declining support to lower the estimated slope, and it may appear that the entire relationship is greater in the earlier era. It may be that the relationships for years 0–10 for the two eras are very different from the simple linear regression. Members in the latter era may be able to exploit the perks of office to rapidly raise their vote percentages. It is possible that the linear relationship for years 0–10 in the latter era is greater, but including all years lowers the overall slope because of a large number of cases of eroding support in the latter years of a career.

This impact of eroding support is a possibility and worth exploring. For this to be the case, it needs to be the case that more members are staying longer and that erosion does set in. It also needs to be the case that the effect is significant enough to lower the linear slope in the latter era below the slope for the earlier era.

The first condition is clearly true. Members are staying longer, and there are many more members who are staying for lengthy careers. Of those members who left by 1945, 5.4 percent of members had a career of 15 years or more. For the years 1946–2006, for those members who had exited, 13.9 percent had stayed 15 years or more. There are more cases of lengthier careers in the latter period.

The second condition is that there is a curvilinear relationship between years in office and vote percentages in both eras and it is more pronounced in the latter era because more members are staying

TABLE 4.3. *The incumbency effect: linear and nonlinear estimations, 1900–2006*

Time period	N	Intercept	Initial %	No. of years	Squared years	R^2
1900–1944						
Linear	9,742	14.5	.76	.55		.55
Nonlinear	9,742	14.3	.76	.72	−.0096	.55
Linear – < 20 yrs	9,607	14.3	.76	.57		.55
1946–2006						
Linear	14,310	30.4	.56	.29		.29
Nonlinear	14,310	28.3	.57	.83	−.02	.30
Linear – < 20 yrs	13,189	27.8	.59	.47		.30

longer. To estimate whether a curvilinear estimation might be a better representation of the relationship between length of time in office and vote percentages, the same equation as that shown in Table 4.2 was run, but with a squared term for "term" added. Table 4.3 presents the following analyses. First, the linear additive model, using the variables of years in office and initial percentage, is presented for the two eras of 1900–1944 and 1946–2006. Then the curvilinear model is presented, adding the squared term for years in office. Then, to remove the effects of the cases in which the vote percentage declines with greater years in office, the linear relationship is run only on those cases in which the term of office was 20 years or less.

The important question is whether a curvilinear estimation produces a better fit than a linear estimation. The test for that is whether the *addition* to the R^2 for the curvilinear model is significantly greater than the addition for the linear estimation (Gujarati, 2003: 260–64). The *F* test of significance for additional variance explained does not indicate for either era that the nonlinear estimation adds significantly to the R^2 compared to the linear estimation. As shown in Table 4.3, substantively, there is little change in the R^2 when a squared term is added within either era.

Nonetheless, there is more of a nonlinear relationship in the years 1946–2006, and it is worth pursuing the difference to see if it somehow makes a difference in how we see the patterns before and after 1945.

Two matters are important. First, does the estimation of a nonlinear pattern for 1946–2006 show a different pattern than for 1900–1944? Second, if the analysis is confined to careers of 20 years or less, to

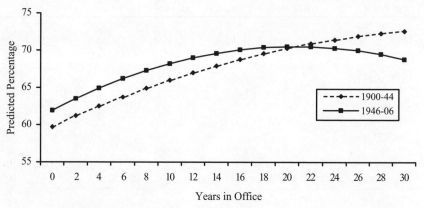

Figure 4.3. Predicted curvilinear vote percentages for incumbents by era.

remove years of declining support, how does the relationship of vote percentage and years in office compare in the two eras?

Figure 4.3 addresses the first question. It presents the plots of the predicted vote percentage, based on the number of years in office, for the nonlinear estimations for the two eras. The initial percentage is set at 60 percent (the typical starting point for incumbents across the century) in the nonlinear equation, and then the predicted vote percentage (using the coefficients from the equations in Table 4.3) is calculated for successive terms.

The relationship for 1946–2006 starts at a higher initial level than for 1900–1944. The 1946–2006 pattern then peaks sooner and begins to decline, while the 1900–1944 trend is still increasing. The peak vote percentage for the latter years is at 20 years, when the predicted vote percentage is 70.5 percent. The net increase in the predicted vote percentage – from initial to peak – for those members with elections in 1946–2006 is less than the net increase for those members running in earlier years. The answer to the first question – whether the patterns differ – is yes.

Given the greater decline in vote percentages in years beyond the 20th year in office for those members running in years 1946–2006, it could be that this decline is bringing down the linear estimation for the years 1946–2006. To eliminate the effect of these later years, a linear estimation was run on both eras, using only years 0–20 of careers within both eras. The result is shown in Table 4.3 for each era in the row "Linear – < 20 yrs." When these elections are removed, the slope for 1946–2006 increases from .29 to .47, but the .47 slope is still less than the slope for the earlier era, which is .57.

In sum, there is more of a nonlinear relationship in the years 1946–2006 between years in office and vote percentage. That difference, however, does not somehow explain the difference in relationships between the two sets of years. During the latter years the relationship between vote percentage and years in office is less, regardless of whether the estimation is linear with all cases included, nonlinear with all cases included, or linear with only cases of 20 years in office or less. This provides further evidence that the situation of incumbents is not better in recent decades than in the years 1900–1944. Indeed, using this measure, incumbents in the current era are worse off.

NET CAREER CHANGES IN VOTE PERCENTAGES

Another way to assess the ability of incumbents to increase their electoral security is to assess the net change in their vote percentages from the beginning to the end of their careers. If incumbents are able to increase their security, they should have a net positive increase in their percentages by the end of their careers. If incumbents are improving their ability to increase their votes, this net gain should be greater for the most recent decades than for earlier decades. To calculate this, the final percentage is subtracted from the initial percentage, whether that was achieved in a special or general election for each career.[14]

---

[14] The beginning of a career is regarded as the first election for office, even if it is a special election. There is also the issue of what constitutes the end of a career. There are complications in marking the last election of an incumbent for any given career. The issues range from conceptual to odd. There are some incumbents who lost in a primary. If general election results are used, these endings cannot be included because primary results are unknown. But the career of an incumbent was ended via an election. When I have discovered that an incumbent did not run for reelection because of a primary loss, I have chosen to use the percentage in the primary when it is available. The Biographical Directory distinguishes primary losses from voluntary retirements by saying the individual "was unsuccessful in seeking renomination." For example, Victor Wickersham, Oklahoma, lost in primaries in 1946, 1956, and 1964. I was able to obtain the primary percentages from Carolyn Hanneman at the Carl Albert Center. If these primary losses were not included, Wickersham would be recorded as voluntarily leaving office three times, when in reality, he lost three times. There are other cases that are odder and difficult to code. Victor Berger was

TABLE 4.4. *Increase in incumbent vote percentages over a career*

| | | Average vote % | | | Distribution of changes | | | |
Years	N	Begin	End	Change	<−10	−10–<0	0–<10	10+
1900–2006	3,867	59.1	58.6	−.5	18.7	38.8	24.6	18.0
1900–1944	1,822	58.8	56.2	−2.5	21.4	40.8	25.7	12.1
1946–2006	2,045	59.4	60.7	1.4	16.3	37.0	23.5	23.2
1946–1964	757	61.0	58.7	−2.2	18.6	47.0	21.3	13.0
1966–2006	1,295	58.6	61.9	3.4	14.9	31.1	24.8	29.2

Table 4.4 presents information on the net changes in vote percentages for all members who were elected in 1900 and after and who had left office by 2006, including those who left voluntarily and those who lost their last elections. Over the last century the average incumbent has been surprisingly ineffective in increasing his or her vote percentage over a career. On average, over the entire time period, incumbents began with a vote percentage of 59.1 percent and left with a percentage of 58.6 percent. Viewed in terms of the distribution of net changes, over half of all incumbents left with a percentage lower than their initial ones.

If changes are grouped into pre- and post-1944, there is evidence that incumbents have been able to modestly improve their vote percentages over time. For the years 1900–1944 the average change was −2.5 percentage points, while for the years 1946–2006, there has been an average positive change of 1.4 percentage points. While

elected as a Socialist from Milwaukee in 1910, and he was seated. He was a seated incumbent who was then defeated in 1912. He ran as a challenger in 1914, and 1916 and lost. He was then elected in 1918 but Congress refused to seat him because of his opposition to World War I. His seat was never filled and in a 1919 special election after Congress refused to seat him, he was again elected, but Congress again refused to seat him. In 1920 he was defeated as an unseated incumbent. He was then elected in 1922, 1924, and 1926 but never seated, and no one took his place. He was then defeated in 1928. There were no special elections from 1922 to 1928 to replace him, and no one else took the seat. He was the incumbent in 1912, 1919, and 1924, 1926, and 1928, but Congress would not accept his credential or seat him. Since no one else took his seat, he is included in this analysis of incumbents as having three careers (1910–12, 1918–1920, and 1922–1928). An equally odd case involves that of Patsy Mink from Hawaii. She was an incumbent during 2002 but died in September 2002. She was left on the ticket and elected after her death. While including her may be a little odd because she was no longer alive, she was on the ballot as an incumbent and is included.

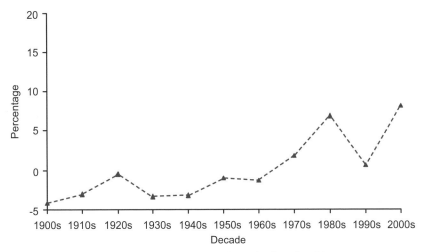

Figure 4.4. Average net change for incumbents by decade of departure, 1900–2006. Data compiled by the author.

incumbents have a net positive increase in their vote percentages since 1946, it is still the case that for those incumbents ending their careers during 1946–2006, 53.2 percent ended their careers with a final percentage lower than their initial percentages. If net changes over the last 60 years are broken down into 1946–1964 and 1966 and after, the evidence indicates more positive changes over time. The average change for 1944–1964 is negative (−2.2), while the average change for 1966–2006 is 3.4.

If the results are organized by the decade of departure, as in Figure 4.4, the evidence is more supportive of the argument that incumbents now have a greater ability to increase their vote percentages. Net changes were generally less than zero until the 1960s, and they have largely been positive since then.

While the prior indicators have not provided evidence of a growing incumbency, the net change indicator does. There are, however, reasons to be cautious about just what this increase represents. The implication is that on average, incumbents are now able to increase their vote percentages during their careers more than in the past. But that conclusion appears to conflict with the results in Table 4.2.

Those results, showing the relationship between years in office and vote percentage, indicate that this relationship is less after 1944.

The resolution of this seeming contradiction – a greater net change in vote percentages but a diminished rate of increase over time – is that incumbents now stay in office longer than they used to. Vote percentages increase with longevity (even if the increase is now less than before), and the greater net increases reflect the increased longevity of members.[15]

Incumbents clearly stay longer now than in the early 1900s (Polsby, 1968). Figure 4.5 indicates the average years in office for incumbents, organized by the decade in which they left office. For the first half of the century, incumbents, on average, stayed much less than 10 years. That average increased from the 1940s through the 1960s and has consistently been about 11–13 years since the 1960s.

If incumbent vote percentages increase on average with successive years in office, as shown earlier, then greater longevity alone would

---

[15] While longevity increases the net career increase of a member, it is worth noting that this impact has declined over time. The following table indicates the results of regressing net career changes on the length of time in office and the initial percentage a member received.

Two matters are important. First, the impact of longevity has declined over time. In effect, those who stayed 10 years before 1946 realized a greater net increase in their vote percentages than those who left after 1946. For the 1965–2006 time period the impact is even less.

Second, the primary effect on net change is the initial percentage of a member. The relationship is negative, indicating that the higher the initial percentage, the less the net increase. Those incumbents who started with a relatively high percentage usually had a net decline by the time they ended. Those incumbents with relatively low initial percentages had the highest net increases.

Effect of longevity, by grouped years, on net career changes for those incumbents ending careers, 1902–2006 (unstandardized regression coefficients)

Years elected	N	Intercept	Initial %	No. of years	R^2
1900–2006	3,885	18.1	−.39	.48	.14
1900–1944	1,830	9.3	−.30	.84	.15
1946–2006	2,055	28.5	−.52	.33	.17
1946–1964	759	18.4	−.41	.44	.17
1965–2006	1,296	35.5	−.60	.23	.17

Unstandardized regression coefficients.

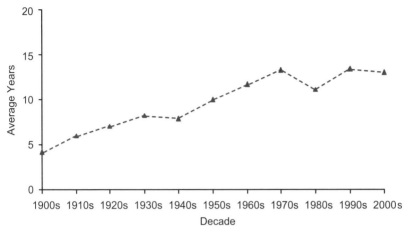

Figure 4.5. Average length of careers in office by decade of departure, 1900–2006. Data compiled by the author.

produce greater net increases in vote percentages for exiting incumbents. Perhaps a more relevant indicator of how incumbents are faring is how incumbents with equivalent years in office but from different eras have fared. Table 4.5 presents this information. For each era, the average net change in vote percentage is calculated for the number of years in office. Incumbents in the last half of the century, for equivalent years in office, generally increased their vote percentages over vote percentages achieved by those serving from 1900 to 1944. For those serving after 1966 the increase for a given number of years in office is slightly greater than for 1900–1944.

While the net increase for years in office is greater for later years, it is again worth noting that the increase for 1966–2006 compared

TABLE 4.5. *Net increases in vote percentage by years in office and years exiting*

| Years in office | Years incumbent left | | | |
	All	1900–1944	1946–2006	1966–2006
4	.51	−.97	.22	.33
8	1.03	−1.15	3.08	4.97
12	1.98	1.38	2.36	4.50
16	2.70	3.96	2.13	4.95

to 1900–1944 is very modest.[16] If the years 1900–1944 are compared with 1966–2006, a 12-year veteran in the latter period experienced a net gain in his or her vote percentage of 2.52 percentage points over the 12-year veteran from the earlier era. A 16-year veteran had a gain of .99 percentage points over what an incumbent in the earlier era might achieve (4.95–3.96). If recent incumbents have been able to increase their vote percentages, it is a remarkably small change.

The evidence presented thus far provides no support for the argument that incumbents are doing better. Their vote percentages have not increased. Their ability to increase their vote percentages with successive years in office is less for 1946–2006 than for 1900–1944. Their net vote increases during their careers are somewhat higher, but only because they stay longer now than in prior years.

[16] It may appear that Tables 4.1–4.4 are in conflict. Table 4.1 presents evidence that the increase in vote percentages for successive years in office is less in 1946–2006 than in 1900–1944. Those results suggest that members who stayed four or eight years in the earlier period would have larger increases (relative to their initial percentages) than those members in the later period. The results in Table 4.4 seem to be in conflict, with larger increases for those members exiting in 1966–2006. The reason for the discrepancy is the analyses' focus on different aspects of the careers of incumbents, and the results should not be expected to be the same. Table 4.1 is about the relationship between years in office and increases in vote percentages, *controlling* for initial percentages. It also represents the general, linear, predicted relationship between years and vote percentage, while Table 4.4 presents net changes only. Furthermore, Table 4.3 presents actual changes for those members exiting after specific years in office and does not involve predicted scores.

CHAPTER 5

The Retirement Slump

A final indicator of the possibility of a growing incumbency effect is the *retirement slump*, or the decline in the partisan vote in a district when an incumbent leaves. If a Republican incumbent received 65 percent in her last election and the Republican candidate in the next election receives 55 percent, then the slump in the Republican percentage is 10 percentage points. This difference is taken as an indication of how much an incumbent was able to boost the vote percentage over what a nonincumbent (the new Republican candidate) would receive. The new vote, without an incumbent present, is taken as the base vote in the district. As noted earlier, numerous studies have found that this retirement slump increased beginning in the 1960s. Figure 5.1 indicates the average retirement slump by decade over the last century for all incumbents who left by 2006.

This evidence indicates that the retirement slump increased significantly beginning in the 1960s. This suggests that incumbents have been able to boost their vote percentages over their careers, as shown in Figure 4.2, resulting in a greater drop in the partisan vote when an incumbent retires.

There are, however, two very significant problems with the indicator. First, it may be biased, excluding many cases of exiting incumbents and picking up primarily the incumbents who were relatively successful. Second, there are reasons to wonder whether it is actually tracking what it purports to measure. Each of these issues deserves attention.

With regard to which exiting incumbents are included, the problem is that the measure as defined excludes a substantial percentage of exits from the House. The "retirement slump is the average vote loss

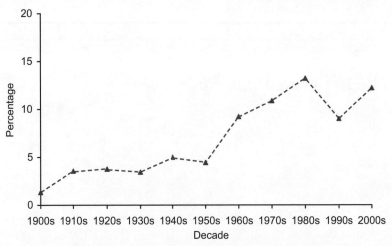

Figure 5.1. Average retirement slump for incumbents by decade of departure, 1900–2006. Data compiled by the author.

for the parties whose candidates won election 1 [the prior election] and did not run in election 2 [the current election]" (Gelman and King, 1990: 1145). The focus in this definition is on those who *voluntarily* leave the House. Many of those exiting do so because they lose. How to deal with these cases presents an interesting and difficult issue, which may have considerable significance for our assessment of the extent of a retirement slump.

As indicated earlier, roughly one-half of all incumbents in the last century exited via a loss, whether in a primary or general election. The percentage of incumbents exiting via a loss was higher in the first half of the century, and it has declined since midcentury. While this percentage has declined, even in the decades of the 1980s–2000s, when a relatively low percentage lost, at least 20 percent of all incumbents left the House through this route.[1]

[1] The decline in exits over time is intriguing. This could be taken as a reflection of the improving fortunes of incumbents. They could be better at warding off electoral defeat, reflecting more success among incumbents in creating electoral security. But it could also be because incumbents in serious trouble are now more aware of that and choose to retire rather than face the stigma of ending their careers through defeat. It could reflect a greater inclination of incumbents to retire on their own terms. The rise of political polling could provide the desired information. For example, in early 2008, with President George Bush very unpopular, opposition to Iraq continuing to be strong and Bush offering very limited reductions in troops, and the economy possibly going into recession under a Republican president, 28 House members had announced their retirement by late January,

Focusing on voluntary exits means analyzing only those members who left on favorable terms. If the goal is to assess changes in partisan vote percentages only under circumstances of favorable exits, then the retirement slump is an appropriate indicator. But if the concern is with what happens to the partisan vote in a district in the transition from having an incumbent present to the next election, the conventional way of assessing this is heavily biased toward creating a positive retirement slump statistic. Excluding the 40 (and perhaps 50) percent who ultimately lose means measuring the more positive cases.[2] Over the last century those incumbents who exited voluntarily began with an average vote percentage of 63.1 and ended with an average of 68.4, for an average gain of 5.3. Those who left via a loss began with an average of 53.3 and ended with an average of 44.2, for a net change of −9.1.

Recognizing this omission may help, but even if we were to try to include cases of a loss, it is not clear how that might be done and still retain some conceptual continuity with the original notion. If incumbent losses are included, we might measure the difference between the last winning election and the next or losing election. This measure would presumably result in a large negative number, reflecting

while only 5 Democrats had. See Carl Hulse and David M. Herszenhorn, "G.O.P. Exodus in House Bodes Ill for Fall Success," *New York Times*, January 31, 2008, http://www.nytimes.com/2008/01/31/us/politics/31house.html. While this could be the case, we do not have much information on when polling became widely accessible and available to congressional candidates or on what prompted an incumbent to retire. We also do not know the polling results in specific districts that might have prompted decisions.

[2] The exclusion occurs as follows. When an analysis of the retirement slump is conducted, an election is classified as having an incumbent present or not. If it is open (no incumbent present), then the partisan vote in the open seat race is compared to the partisan vote of the incumbent from two years prior. If a Republican held the seat in 1982 but does not run in 1984, then the Republican incumbent vote in 1982 is compared to that received by the Republican in 1984. The difference (presumably positive) is the slump. If the Republican incumbent was defeated in 1982 by a Democratic incumbent, in 1984 the district is coded as having a Democratic incumbent and is not deemed relevant for any analysis of the retirement slump. The cases in which an incumbent loses are, in effect, lost in this pairing of cases across years. An incumbent exits, but the transition from an incumbent percentage to a nonincumbent percentage is not considered. We are left with cases in which an incumbent chose to leave voluntarily. Since the incumbent won, the percentage is presumably relatively high, so the slump is likely to be positive. While it is not clear how to deal with these cases, the decision to include only those voluntarily leaving misses some important cases. In years like 1964, 1974, 1994, and 2006, when many incumbents lost, this means that many cases of a transition in party strength are just excluded.

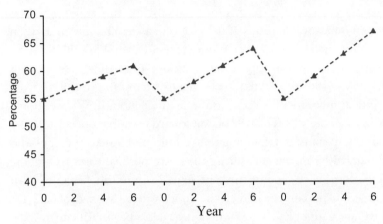

Figure 5.2. Successive hypothetical patterns of incumbent: Open-seat vote percentages.

the drop in the incumbent's percentage. The difficulty with this measure is that it does not involve the change in the partisan vote from an incumbent to a challenger. We could also compare the last vote of a losing incumbent (say, a Republican) and the Republican vote in the next election, but since a new Democratic incumbent would be present, we would be comparing the vote of a losing Republican incumbent with that of a Republican challenger of an incumbent. The idea of comparing an exiting incumbent with a nonincumbent situation would be lost.

Neither approach seems very satisfactory. The retirement slump measure, then, should be viewed with considerable caution. It does show a clear rise beginning in the 1960s, but it is a selective measure of changes after *some* incumbents leave.

Aside from this problem of which cases are being examined, there are also reasons to wonder just what the retirement slump is picking up. While it is never articulated, the general premise of the retirement slump indicator appears to be that there is some stable partisan vote in a district that the incumbent changes, and then the vote returns to its initial level. The difference from the stable vote is the retirement slump.

Figure 5.2 illustrates this. An incumbent, running in an open seat, begins with 55 percent of the vote. Over time she raises her vote

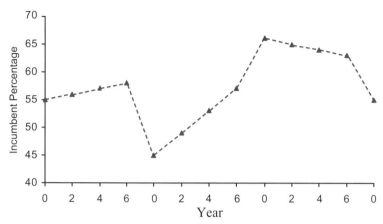

Figure 5.3. Other hypothetical patterns of incumbent: Open-seat vote percentages.

percentage from 55 to 57 to 59 and then to 61. She retires, and the vote returns to 55. The retirement slump is 61–55, or 6. The next incumbent is more successful in raising his percentage, and he increases it in successive elections to 58, 61, and then 64. When he retires and the seat is open, and the partisan vote returns to its normal level (not influenced by an incumbent) of 55, the retirement slump is now 64–55, or 9. The next incumbent raises her percentage even more (from 55 to 59 to 63 to 67), and the retirement slump grows to 67–55, or 12.

The presumption here is that there is some so-called normal (for the district) vote percentage that the vote returns to when the incumbent leaves. If so, then the retirement slump reflects the change in the vote due to the presence or absence of an incumbent. An increasing retirement slump reflects greater incumbent success. But what if the vote percentages after an incumbent retires differ from this generally unstated presumed base or stable vote? Figure 5.3 presents three possible sequences. In the first case (the first five data points in the graph) the incumbent increases his vote percentage from 55 to 56 to 57 to 58, or a total of 3 percentage points. When he retires, the partisan vote percentage for the same party as the incumbent drops to 45. The incumbent increased his vote percentage three points, but the retirement slump is 13 because the partisan vote did not return to

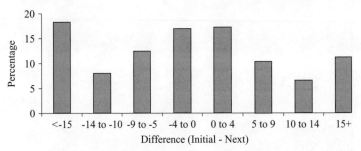

Figure 5.4. Differences between initial incumbent percentage: Next open-seat percentage, 1900–2006.

55, but went to 45. In this case, most of the retirement slump number is not a reflection of the ability of the incumbent to affect the vote. Most of the change is due to some shift in the partisan vote in the district.

The next incumbent begins at 45, and moves to 49, 53, and 57. When she retires, the partisan vote percentage moves to 66, and her retirement slump is −9, even though she increased her vote by 12 percentage points. Finally, the third incumbent, who began at 66, moves to 65, then 64, and then 63. He then retires and the vote drops to 55, resulting in a retirement slump of 8, even though the incumbent steadily lost support while in office.

These sequences are, of course, hypothetical, but they represent cases where specific retirement slump numbers are quite suspect as to what they are capturing. The first case creates an impression of a considerable retirement slump when the incumbent had a modest effect. The second reflects a case where the incumbent achieved a significant increase in her vote but has a negative retirement slump. The third represents a case where an incumbent has a high retirement slump number but actually lost electoral support while in office.

The question is whether these hypothetical cases are common or occasional flukes. To what extent do district vote percentages return to the level that existed when an incumbent first ran for office? Figure 5.4 indicates the distribution of changes from the vote percentage when an incumbent first ran in an open seat to when the seat was next open, for cases in which an incumbent voluntarily retired. A negative number means the vote percentage for the same party declined from the first election of an incumbent to the next open-seat race. A positive number means the partisan vote increased. Over the last century, roughly 34 percent of cases involved a situation in which the vote percentage after the incumbent left was within ±5 percentage points of the initial percentage the exiting incumbent received; that is, only one-third returned to a level reasonably close to that which prevailed when the incumbent first ran. For 29 percent of the cases the first open-seat percentages were either 15 points lower or 15 points higher than the initial percentage. Forty-four percent of cases were either 10 points less or 10 points more than the initial vote percentage.

For almost two-thirds of incumbents, there was a decline or an increase of 5 percentage points or more from one open-seat election to another. These open-seat to open-seat fluctuations are very important for calculations of the retirement slump. The concept of the retirement slump seems simple, measuring the drop (change) in the partisan vote from one election to the next. But the calculation is affected by the shift in the district's partisan vote from one open seat to the next. If someone starts at 55, goes to 60, and then, in the next open-seat election, the partisan vote drops to 50, the retirement slump is 60–50, or 10. Five points of the slump are due to a partisan vote shift.

Table 5.1 presents examples of just how much the latter change can matter. The first set involves incumbents who experienced a decline in their vote percentages during their careers but ended up with a positive retirement slump because the partisan vote in the district declined significantly by the next open-seat election. The second set involves members who, despite increasing their vote percentages during their careers, had a negative retirement slump because the partisan vote increased in the next election.

These are just examples of how much the open-seat to open-seat change can matter. In any data set that encompasses over 2,000 cases, such examples can probably be found. The question is how typical such examples are and whether there has been some change over time in open-seat to open-seat shifts that might affect the calculation of the retirement slump. Table 5.2 presents a summary of how changes in partisan votes from one open seat to the next open seat affect the retirement slump. Retirements are organized by the extent of change from one open seat to the next. Those districts in which there has

TABLE 5.1. *Examples of career vote changes and retirement slumps*

Name/District	Year left	Years in office	First	Last	Change	Next	Shift	Slump
						Percentage		
Negative career change, negative open-seat to open-seat change, positive retirement slump								
Crail – CA 10	1932	6	87.0	75.0	−12.0	44.7	−42.3	30.2
Rich – PA 16	1942	12	75.5	60.5	−15.0	48.7	−26.8	11.8
Dorn – SC 3	1974	28	99.9	75.2	−24.7	61.8	−38.1	13.4
Hutto – FL 1	1994	16	63.3	52.0	−11.3	39.0	−24.3	13.0
Positive career change, positive open-seat to open-seat change, negative retirement slump								
McKenzie – Il 13	1924	14	61.3	70.0	8.7	77.8	16.5	−7.8
Douglass – MA 11	1934	10	58.9	85.7	26.7	99.9	41.0	−14.3
Gingrich – GA 6	1998	20	54.4	58.0	3.6	71.0	16.6	−13.0
Lamson – TX 9	2004	8	53.0	58.6	5.6	72.2	19.2	−13.6

TABLE 5.2. *Distribution of open-seat to next-open-seat percentages and retirement slumps by category, 1900–1944 and 1946–2006*

	−5% or Less	−5–0%	0–5%	5% or More
1900–1944				
Number of cases	288	154	217	283
% of all cases	30.5	16.3	23.0	30.0
Initial %	66.6	63.6	72.5	57.0
Ending %	62.0	65.4	74.4	70.0
Net career % change	−4.6	1.8	1.9	13.0
Next open %	50.2	61.5	74.4	72.8
Change open to next open	−16.4	−2.1	1.9	15.8
Retirement slump	11.8	3.9	.0	−2.8
1946–2006				
Number of cases	542	240	186	368
% of all cases	40.5	18.0	13.9	27.5
Initial %	67.1	59.3	62.2	55.9
Ending %	67.2	65.9	68.3	72.5
Net career % change	.1	6.7	6.1	16.5
Next open %	48.7	56.8	64.5	72.7
Change open to next open	−18.5	−2.5	2.2	16.8
Retirement slump	18.5	9.2	3.9	−.3

been a significant decrease in partisan percentages from one open seat to the next are presented first. Those with a significant increase in the partisan vote from one open seat to the next are to the far right. The results are presented by pre-1946 and after to allow an assessment of relationships within eras and what has changed across time.

Several matters are important. First, focusing on the years 1900–1944, there is a strong relationship between the average open-seat to open-seat change (the variation across the four columns) and the average retirement slump.[3] In the left column are those seats where

3 There is also a strong association between the net career change of an incumbent and the retirement slump. Those incumbents who experience a larger net increase also have larger retirement slumps. Both the net career change and the open-seat to open-seat change matter. The bivariate association between net career change and open-seat to open-seat change is .50. Larger net career changes are associated with large increases in the partisan vote percentage from one open seat to another. The correlation of net career changes with the retirement slump is .46, and the correlation of open-seat to open-seat changes is −.54. These associations mean that as net career changes increase, the pattern is that the subsequent partisan vote percentage is higher. A net career change increases the retirement slump, and the accompanying positive open-seat partisan change suppresses change. Why these patterns prevail is taken up later.

the greatest decline in open-seat to open-seat percentages occurred. These seats also have the greatest retirement slump. In contrast, in the right column are the cases in which the open-seat change is positive and the retirement slump is negative. The pattern is that a high retirement slump occurs in cases in which the partisan vote declines from one open seat to the next.

Second is the relationship between the retirement slump and the net vote percentage increase for incumbents during their career. The highest retirement slump occurs for incumbents who had a negative net increase in their vote percentages over a career. The lowest *and negative* retirement slump occurs for incumbents who had a positive net career percentage increase. In the former cases, where the open-seat to open-seat decline is -5 or below, the net career change is -4.6 percent and the average retirement slump is at its greatest (11.8). The largest retirement slumps occurred when incumbents experienced declines in their careers. When incumbents experienced an average vote percentage increase of 13.0 during their careers (right column), the average open-seat to open-seat increase was 15.8 percentage points, resulting in a retirement slump of -2.8. The point is important: those who experienced an increase in their vote percentage over their career tended to end up with negative retirement slumps. Open-seat to open-seat changes significantly affect the resulting retirement slump score.

Third, and important for understanding why the retirement slump has increased over time, is the distribution of cases in 1946–2006 compared to 1990–1944. In 1900–1944, 53.0 percent of all cases of retirement involved situations in which the changes in percentages from one open seat to the next were positive. An increase in the partisan vote percentage from one open seat to the next lowers the retirement slump. The majority of cases were positive, which means the average retirement slump was reduced. Given that the average net career change during these years was modest (as noted earlier), the distribution of open-seat changes acted to have a modest effect on reducing the calculated retirement slump.

In the years 1946–2006 the same general relationship between open-seat changes, retirement slumps, and net career changes also exists. Higher retirement slumps exist in those districts with a

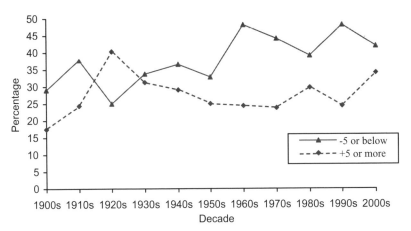

Figure 5.5. Distribution of positive and negative changes from open-seat to next by decade, 1900–2006.

significant open-seat to open-seat change. The difference in the later years is in the overall distribution of open-seat changes. While 47.0 percent were negative in the earlier years, in the second half of the century, 58.5 percent of cases are negative. With more cases in the 1946–2006 years of a retiring incumbent being followed by a decline in the partisan vote, the result is more cases in which the retirement slump is increased. If average net career changes were unchanged from the years 1900–1944, the open-seat to open-seat changes alone would produce a greater retirement slump.

The timing of the shift toward more declines in open-seat to open-seat changes is particularly important. The major increase in the retirement slump occurred in the 1960s and has persisted roughly since then. Figure 5.5 tracks the percentage of open-seat to open-seat changes that were below −5 percentage points and those that were 5 percentage points or greater by decade. The percentage of positive cases (increases in open-seat to open-seat percentages) has remained relatively constant over time. During the 1960s the percentage of cases with declines of below −5 increased significantly, and that percentage has stayed relatively high since then.

The effect of relatively more cases of open-seat to open-seat decreases in partisan percentages beginning in the 1960s is to increase the average retirement slump. Some of the retirement slump increase is due to the greater average net career increase (Figure 4.2), but the greater frequency of decreases in the partisan vote from one open seat to another has played a significant role in increasing the apparent retirement slump. Why there has been an increase in partisan shifts from one open seat to the next open seat will be taken up later. The important matter at this point is that there are reasons to doubt the utility of the retirement slump as an indicator of an increased incumbency effect. There are also reasons to doubt that the increase in the retirement slump beginning in the 1960s reflects the ability of incumbents to move the vote. It may also reflect something about changes in partisan voting patterns in American politics.

A SUMMARY OF THE EVIDENCE

The argument that the incumbency effect has increased is based on changes over time for several indicators. The presumed changes are as follows:

- The average vote percentage of incumbents has increased.
- The ability to increase the vote with successive years in office has increased.
- The net increase in the vote from the beginning to the end of careers has increased.
- The retirement slump has increased.

Each of these conclusions is not supported by the evidence. The average vote percentage of incumbents has not increased from 1946 to 2006. The ability to increase the vote percentage with successive years in office is less for the years 1946–2006 than for 1900–1944. The net increase in the vote percentages of incumbents over their careers has increased in recent decades, but almost all of that increase is due to the greater length of time they stay, and not the ability to increase the vote. Finally, much of the apparent increase in the retirement slump is because partisan voting in districts is shifting significantly from one open-seat contest to the next. In short, there is little if any evidence to support the conclusion that there has been an increase in the incumbency effect in recent decades.

PART II

Realignment and the Fortunes of (Some) Incumbents

CHAPTER 6

An Alternative Framework: The Role of Realignment

If the evidence of an increased incumbency effect is not convincing, does that mean that nothing happened regarding the electoral fortunes of incumbents? That is not the argument of this analysis. Indeed, there have been two changes involving incumbents, and both are important for understanding the electoral trends of recent decades. The first issue involves which incumbents have improved their situation. Over the last century, there has been a remarkable, long-term political realignment. Democrats dominated House elections from 1932 through 1992. That prompted a focused effort by Republicans to expand their electoral base, eventuating in their takeover of the House in 1995. As this realignment unfolded, it resulted in the improvement of the fortunes of Republican incumbents, but not in the improvement of the fortunes of Democratic incumbents. As Republican fortunes improved, their vote percentages and electoral safety increased, while those of Democrats did not. The change in incumbent fortunes has been partisan, benefiting one party and not the other. The focus on all incumbents missed that differential effect and portrayed change as general, as almost apolitical or nonpartisan. Instead, change was partisan, benefiting one party and not the other.

The second change involved all incumbents and was also a product of realignment. The process of change resulted in many districts changing their voting inclinations. That change created the *appearance* of incumbents becoming safer, even though they were not. When incumbents left office as realignment was occurring, there were often swings in partisan support within districts, which were seen as an increase in the retirement slump. The large changes occurring were really partisan shifts in district inclinations.

This chapter provides an overview of the extent of realignment that has occurred over time, and how Republican fortunes have changed. In Chapter 7 the major incumbency effect indicators are then examined from a partisan, realignment perspective. The focus is on how the fortunes of Republican incumbents changed over time and how that affected the overall indicators. Then Chapter 8 returns to the realignment perspective and explains how those changes eventually brought about greater electoral security for Republicans. Finally, Chapter 9 explains how these changes created the impression of an increased retirement slump, but they really were a product of electoral change.

EXPLAINING POLITICAL CHANGE
IN INCUMBENT SITUATIONS

There are essentially two ways to think about the situation of incumbents and how electoral changes affect them. One posits that elections are largely local and decentralized affairs, with candidates operating independently with their own resources. The emphasis is on candidates, their resources, their opponents, and the interaction with a specific political context. It is largely cross-sectional in nature, focusing on varying situations within a year, with an acknowledgment of shifting year-to-year partisan sentiments. A second approach focuses on broad change over time (Sinclair, 1982). The concern is party positions and national reactions to parties, and how electoral change over time affects the congruence of presidential and House results.

The former view, the candidate-centered view of elections, can be briefly summarized. House incumbents seek to increase their vote percentages (Mayhew, 1974b). Beginning in the 1960s, the political context began to change, with fewer voters identifying with a party and more of them splitting their ticket among party candidates. Members of Congress were acquiring more publicly funded office resources that allowed them to serve constituents and promote themselves to constituents. They could use direct mail to communicate with constituents and polling to assess their success in creating a personal image as an effective and highly visible legislator. Campaigns became centered around the individual candidate, became more personal in nature and less partisan (Fenno, 1978), and the result was an increase in the vote percentages of incumbents. If the availability of resources is central to the success of incumbents, then it seems fairly clear that the electoral security of incumbents should be steadily improving.

In stark contrast is a view that puts partisanship and realignment at the center of an explanation of electoral fortunes. The argument can be summarized briefly. House incumbents are likely to be safer and have higher vote percentages when they are running in districts favorably inclined to their party. To the extent that incumbents are being elected in districts that are won by presidential candidates of the other party, they are less likely to be safe. Electoral alignments and changes in the alignment of presidential and House results play a significant role in which of these two conditions prevails. If a presidential candidate successfully seeks a new constituency with different interests than the existing electoral base of the party, it can create a disjuncture in the electoral bases of the presidential and House parties. The policy stances that create success in the new base may alienate the old base, leaving existing incumbents running in districts less sympathetic to their interests. Only when older incumbents in "older" areas eventually retire, and the House candidates begin to win where presidential candidates are winning, will consistency of partisan outcomes be created. That will put more incumbents in districts sympathetic to their party, and more incumbents will be electorally safe. The greater the overlap between presidential and House results, the greater the number of safe seats the party has.

From the realignment perspective the electoral security of incumbents depends on how realignment is proceeding and in which type of district incumbents are running. If an incumbent's district is won by his or her presidential candidate, the incumbent's situation will likely be fairly safe. If an incumbent is running in a district being won by the presidential candidate of the other party, the incumbent's situation is much less likely to be safe. The most complex and interesting situation is that in which an incumbent's district is changing from one party to another. As will be shown later, it is in this situation that change may create the impression of an increased incumbency effect.

While these two perspectives might be seen as being in conflict, they are not. The candidate-centered view is largely focused on who wins and by how much within a given year. The emphasis is on who has the most money and visibility, and whether a quality challenger exists. Time is incorporated only in terms of the national partisan swing from the prior election and perhaps the number of years an incumbent has been in office. The focus is on average effects, such as the average effect of the presidential vote, of money spent, and the differential in money spent. There is no doubt that all of these matters are very important in any given year (Jacobson, 2001: 21–55). Having more money and visibility than a challenger helps a great deal. Having a supportive partisan presidential vote in the district, on average, produces a higher partisan vote for an incumbent. The limitation of this approach is that it focuses on variations within a year, but the implications are extrapolated to form generalizations across years.

The realignment perspective is much less concerned with variations in these matters within a given year. The focus is on electoral change over time. Situations within any given year are of interest if they embody districts where change is occurring or likely to occur because a House district outcome is in conflict with a presidential outcome. Each perspective explains something different. Cross-sectional studies largely explain winners and losers and margins of victory at one time, while the realignment concern is change, where it is occurring, and with what effect on electoral outcomes.

Regardless, the candidate-centered view *suggests* that the incumbency advantage should be increasing because incumbents have more resources at their disposal, while the realignment view suggests that the crucial matter is the state of realignment in the political process and how it is evolving in specific districts.

UNANSWERED QUESTIONS

Articulating the idea that realignment is occurring and that change has created the appearance of an increased incumbency effect does not explain why the fortunes of the Republican Party in general have improved in House elections. For various reasons, over much of the last century, Republicans were in a weaker electoral situation than Democrats. The emergence of the New Deal coalition in 1932 accentuated that. After that, the Republican Party was a party seeking to alter its minority status in American politics and seeking to oppose the policies of the Democratic Party. As the minority party for much of the century, Republicans were trying to attract new constituents and create a majority. The process of party candidates and leaders trying to change a party's electoral base is not easy, and there is continual uncertainty about what policy directions to pursue to expand a base (Sanders, 1999; James, 2000; Ware, 2006).

Just how they did so is beyond the scope of this analysis, but the party did succeed (Brewer and Stonecash, 2009), and it did change its electoral base over time. It lost seats in its longtime base of the Northeast but gained seats in the growing South. It attracted conservatives, many of whom had been in the Democratic Party in the South. It attracted many more of those constituents with strong religious attachments (Brewer and Stonecash, 2006). These developments corresponded with changes in the electoral base of the Democratic Party, which expanded its base of minority voters and gained seats in the Northeast (Ware, 2006). Over the last century, both parties have transformed their electoral bases. The process of the Republican Party trying to expand its electoral base and reverse its situation produced gains for Republicans in their electoral situation and not for Democrats. Whatever improvement in incumbent fortunes occurred was partisan and realized by Republicans.

The following provides only an overview of the realignment of the last century. This is not a book on realignment, as that story is covered well in other analyses (Black and Black, 1987, 2002; Jacobson, 2003; Stonecash, Brewer, and Mariani, 2003; Polsby, 2004; Brewer and Stonecash, 2006; Jacobson, 2007). We have much more research to do to understand realignment well. The concern here is the effect of realignment on incumbent vote percentages.

SHIFTING REPUBLICAN FORTUNES

The fortunes of political parties are never constant. A party may possess a majority but find that events and social change cost them support

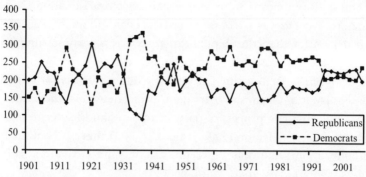

Figure 6.1. House members by party, 1901–2007.

among their existing electoral base, forcing them to try to rebuild their support. They may also be forced to cope with the emergence of new constituencies that change the composition of the electorate. Seeking inroads into that new constituency may conflict with efforts to revitalize the party's older electoral base. Over the last century, Republicans have faced these challenges, and their process of responding to them was lengthy but ultimately successful. That success created the impression of the presumed increase in the incumbency effect.

As the 1900s began, the Republican Party was in a relatively good position with regard to House elections. Following the prolonged disputes of the late 1800s about the role government should play in affecting the availability of credit, the regulation of railroads and business, and the extent of tariffs (Sundquist, 1983: 106–69; Bensel, 2000), Republicans began the 1900s with a solid majority in the House of Representatives. The party largely interpreted the results from the turn of the century as indicating support for its policies of embracing capitalism, restraining the growth of credit, and maintaining many tariffs. As Figure 6.1[1] indicates, for the sessions from 1901 to 1931, Republicans held a majority in the House for all years except 1911– 1916. The party enjoyed strong support in the Northeast and Midwest, which was where the bulk of the population lived.

In the early 1900s, Democrats were acutely aware of their minority status and were continually proposing policies to seek to broaden their

---

[1] Results are taken from U.S. House of Representatives, "Party Divisions," http:// clerk.house.gov/histHigh/Congressional_History/partyDiv.html.

appeal to labor and cities in the North (Sanders, 1999). The party, however, could not shake its image as southern and unreceptive to the influx of European immigrants populating northern cities. Indeed, the party's endeavor in 1928 to present a northern urban presidential candidate, Al Smith, then governor of New York, indicated the party's dilemma. Nominating a candidate like Smith resulted in electoral gains in northern cities (Degler, 1964) but significant losses in presidential support in the South. If the party was too explicit in pursuing one constituency (urban ethnics), it might lose support in its long-standing base of the South.

The Democratic dilemma was largely resolved by the Great Depression and President Herbert Hoover's reaction to it. As the Great Depression unfolded, with employment and incomes rapidly declining, Hoover argued that it would be wrong for the party to intervene in the economy (Sundquist, 1983: 199–204). The result was a 52-seat surge toward Democrats in the 1930 elections, a further 97-seat gain in 1932, and additional gains in 1934 and 1936. From the 1928 to the 1936 elections, Republicans lost a total of 182 seats.

The Great Depression had a remarkable impact on each party. Democrats had struggled for years to build a base beyond the South, and suddenly, they had their traditional southern base plus a new northern urban immigrant base, creating the New Deal coalition. There was a tremendous increase in voter registrations and engagements in northern urban cities, and almost all that vote went for Democrats (Andersen, 1979). This new majority party had its tensions, to be sure. The new liberal wing in the North eventually pushed for civil rights legislation to protect southern blacks and legislation to expand the role of the federal government. That alienated southerners and provided an opening for Republicans to seek southern votes beginning in the 1960s. Taking advantage of this tension within the Democratic Party took some time, however.

For Republicans, what had been a fairly consistent majority in the House of Representatives abruptly evaporated. As Figure 6.1 indicates, the party had brief moments when it reacquired power, such as 1946 and 1952, but these gains did not persist. For 58 of the 62 years from 1933 through 1995 the Republican Party was the minority party in the House. The movement of substantial segments of the electorate

TABLE 6.1. *The electoral security of incumbents by eras and party*

Years/Region	Democrats			Republicans		
	N	% Vote	% Safe	N	% Vote	% Safe
1900–1930						
All	2,564	71.6	57.6	2,949	61.6	43.6
Non-South	1,212	57.5	27.5	2,854	61.0	43.6
South	1,352	84.3	84.6	95	63.1	45.3
1932–1944						
All	1,654	71.8	59.9	947	59.1	34.7
Non-South	1,034	61.2	40.8	929	59.0	34.3
South	620	89.4	91.6	18	65.2	55.6

Ns refer to the number of elections in which an incumbent was present.
Source: Data compiled by the author.

to identify with the Democratic Party affected not only the number of Republicans, but the electoral security of their remaining incumbents. The elections of the 1930s made a weak party situation worse. Despite generally having a majority in the House from 1900 to 1930, Republican incumbents were not very secure electorally, and the elections of the 1930s only made things worse for them. The Republican Party was based almost exclusively in the North, with very few seats in the South. Elections in the North were more competitive than in the South, so Republican incumbents during the years 1900–1930 had closer elections than Democrats. Democratic incumbents, with most of their seats in the South, where one party dominated, enjoyed larger electoral margins.

Table 6.1 indicates the average vote percentages for Democratic and Republican incumbents for 1900–1930 and 1932–1964 for the nation and by South[2] and non-South. During 1900–1930 Democratic incumbents won higher average percentages of the vote (71.6 to 61.6) than Republican incumbents and had a higher percentage of safe seats (57.6 to 43.6), but that was largely due to their strength in the South. Outside the South, where almost all Republican seats were located, Republican incumbents won higher percentages of the vote (61.0 to 57.5) and had a higher percentage of safe seats (43.6 to 27.5).

[2] The South is defined here as Alabama, Florida, Georgia, Kentucky, Louisiana, Mississippi, North Carolina, South Carolina, Tennessee, Texas, and Virginia.

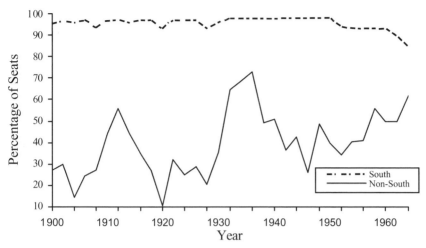

Figure 6.2. Percentage of U.S. House seats won by Democrats by region, 1900–1964. Data are from regional voting results presented in Jerrold G. Rusk, *A Statistical History of the American Electorate* (Washington, DC: CQ Press, 2001), Table 5–8, and compiled by the author.

The 1932 elections altered the relative electoral security of the parties. The primary change was that Democrats increased their success outside the South. From 1900 through 1930 Democrats were largely stuck at winning 30 percent of the seats outside the South. The exception was when the Progressive movement took votes from Republicans in the early 1910s, a disruption that did not last long. As Figure 6.2 indicates, beginning in 1932, Democrats acquired a substantial block of seats outside the South, giving the party a relatively stable majority in the House. Even though the party's remarkable success level in the 1930s did not persist, from 1932 to 1964 Democrats rarely returned to the percentage of nonsouthern seats they had won from 1900 to 1930.

While Democratic fortunes improved significantly beginning in 1932, Republicans not only lost seats, but the incumbents remaining were receiving a smaller percentage of the vote, and a smaller percentage of their incumbents were safe. The significance of these declines for Republicans should not be understated. When a party loses a national election, it is generally reduced to those seats in areas where the party is strongest: its electoral base. It loses seats in marginal or competitive areas, so the remaining incumbents should be in a *relatively* strong situation. The 1930s left Republicans with a much smaller House delegation, and those Republicans remaining were not in a strong electoral situation. The party was not in good shape.

THE REPUBLICAN DILEMMA

While Republicans occasionally won back the House after the 1930s, the party was clearly struggling. By the 1950s, that status was creating internal debates about its future. There were reasons to be discouraged and reasons to be encouraged. Discouragement arose from the view that the party seemed to be in almost permanent minority status in the House and had lost the presidency five consecutive times from 1932 through 1948. They had recruited Dwight Eisenhower, a general returning from World War II, to run as their successful presidential candidate in 1952, but it was unclear if he represented a resurgence of the party or simply the embracing of a popular returning war hero.

The unease about Republicans' status prompted an internal debate about what direction the party should take. The debate was largely between pragmatic moderates and more ideological conservatives. Eisenhower's victories in 1952 and 1956 were seen by many as evidence of the path the party should follow. He was a moderate Republican, largely accepting the broad array of programs enacted during the 1930s. He was pro-business, but not ideological in his commitment to capitalism and reduced taxation. The pragmatists wanted to win elections, and they thought that adopting a moderate stance was the best way to do that.

The other wing of the party comprised conservatives who strongly believed that the party had lost its way as a voice advocating the conservative principles of limited domestic government, reliance on capitalism and individualism, and strong national defense (Rae, 1989: 29–43; Brennan, 1995: 5–7; Hodgson, 1996). Not only did they believe in these principles, but they argued that the only way the party could be an attractive electoral alternative to Democrats was to present the party as representing a different set of principles.

Some conservatives also saw evidence that the party could succeed with a more conservative message. For decades the party had not done

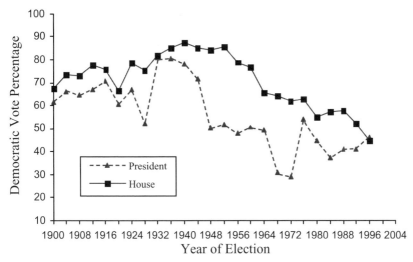

Figure 6.3. Overall vote percentage within the South for Democratic House and presidential candidates, 1900–2004. Data are from Jerrold G. Rusk, *A Statistical History of the American Electorate* (Washington, DC: CQ Press, 2001), 139–40.

well in the South in House elections, but there, some saw signs this might be changing. In 1948 President Truman took a stronger stand than any prior Democrat in favor of civil rights for blacks (Gardner, 2003). As Figure 6.3 indicates, his actions alienated southern voters, and there was a significant drop in political support within the South for Truman. That decline in support for Democratic presidential candidates persisted in the presidential elections involving the Republican candidates Dwight Eisenhower, Richard Nixon, and Barry Goldwater. Conservatives argued that these results provided evidence that Republicans could acquire more support within the South.

There were also signs that the high levels of support Democratic House candidates had enjoyed were eroding. Republican candidates were not winning many House seats, but the overall Democratic percentage of the House vote within the South declined from 84 percent in 1948 to 65 percent in 1964. Some party members were simultaneously arguing for a more conservative direction and eyeing their success in the South, always seen as more conservative (Black and Black, 1987), as proof that their message would win them votes in an area that had previously been written off by the party.

The mid-1960s marked a significant turning point for the party. Senator Barry Goldwater, representing frustration with Eisenhower's acceptance of the role of government established during the New Deal of the 1930s, had emerged as a leader of the conservative wing of the party in the late 1950s. Conservatives were able to nominate Barry Goldwater as their presidential candidate in 1964. His run in 1964 failed badly, and many Republican House members lost as a result of his campaign. Democrats gained so many seats outside the South that they were able to enact new federal programs such as Medicaid and Medicare in 1965–1968.

While moderates within the party saw their losses in 1964 as an indication that they must pursue a moderate path, the burst of liberal legislation after 1964 was proof to many conservative Republicans that they needed to mobilize to oppose the growth of government in American society. They saw a greater federal government as more intrusive and as detrimental to preserving freedom in American society. Perhaps most important, the conservatives whom Goldwater had recruited for the 1964 campaign remained in many party positions following the election, and they worked to recruit and elect more conservatives. While there was considerable commentary after the 1964 election that conservatives were now less significant in American politics, having had their ideas rejected in the election, conservatives were renewing their efforts to organize so to advocate for their views (Edwards, 1999; Perlstein, 2001). Subsequent Republican presidential candidates, such as Richard Nixon and Ronald Reagan, saw the potential of seeking votes in the South to improve their chances of winning presidential elections and a majority in Congress (Phillips, 1969; Carter, 1995: 324–414).

The Republican efforts to attract more conservatives set off a sustained realignment in American politics, with presidential candidates leading the way (Stonecash, 2007). Republican presidential candidates made inroads into the South well before the party's House candidates had much success (Black and Black, 1987, 2002). Gradually, Republican House candidates caught up to the success of presidential candidates and were able to achieve electoral support equivalent to what presidential candidates were achieving. The Republican Party

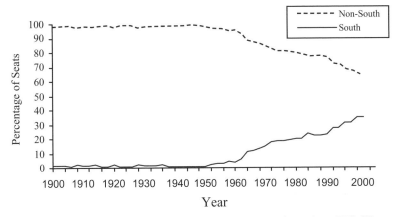

Figure 6.4. Percentage of Republican seats from each region, U.S. House, 1900–2006. Data are from regional voting results presented in Jerrold G. Rusk, *A Statistical History of the American Electorate* (Washington, DC: CQ Press, 2001), Table 5–8, and compiled by the author.

was gradually attracting more and more conservatives to their side (Stonecash, 2007), particularly so in the South (Black and Black, 2002). The party became more conservative in its desire to limit the fiscal role of government, but also in its desire to support traditional ways of living (Dionne, 1997: 199–299; Green et al., 1998; Brewer and Stonecash, 2007: 87–162).

This success had its negative consequences. Adopting more conservative positions and winning southern seats cost the party seats in the rest of the country. As Figure 6.4 indicates, the party was gradually replacing support outside the South with support inside the South. In New England, for example, the party has steadily lost its dominance, and after the 2006 elections, there was one remaining Republican House member from that region.

The transformation in the party's electoral base over the last century has been considerable. To return to Figure 6.3, the party has gone from almost no success in the South in House elections to winning over 50 percent of all elections in that region. At the same time, the region has grown enormously in population, creating a region with more House seats for the party (Black and Black, 1992). The argument that the party could present a conservative message and win seats in a region seen as conservative has proved to be correct.

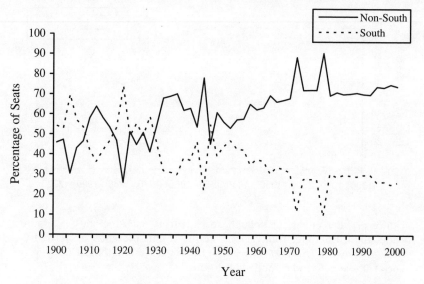

Figure 6.5. Percentage of Democratic House seats derived from regions, 1900–2006.

The Democratic Party was also experiencing significant changes. As it lost seats in the South, it was becoming more dependent on seats outside the South. Figure 6.5 indicates how the transition for the party has proceeded. The party has gone through two waves of change. In the 1930s the party abruptly acquired many more seats outside the South. It retained its southern seats, but they became a smaller part of the House party. Then, beginning in the 1950s, the party gradually lost its dominance in the South, resulting in a growing reliance on seats outside the South. By the early 2000s, only about 25 percent of its seats came from the South.

REALIGNMENT AND THE CONSEQUENCES FOR INCUMBENTS

The important matter is how this realignment affected the fortunes of incumbents. Over the last century the Republican and Democratic parties have made remarkable transitions in their electoral bases. Republicans once had few seats in the South, but their presidential candidates

TABLE 6.2. *Electoral success of House incumbents by electoral success of their presidential candidates, 1900–2004 (presidential years only)*

Republican incumbents				Democratic incumbents			
Presidential %	N	House vote %	% Members safe	Presidential %	N	House vote %	% Members safe
0–39	350	55.6	26.2	0–39	681	66.9	49.8
40–49	740	58.8	33.7	40–49	1,226	64.9	50.7
50–59	1,486	61.5	46.1	50–59	1,316	67.2	58.7
60+	1,460	68.2	81.3	60+	1,784	82.6	95.1

made inroads there beginning in the 1950s, and House candidates eventually followed. For many years the Democratic Party did not do well in the Northeast and New England and now does very well there.

The argument of this analysis is a relatively simple one. This realignment created changes in the electoral security of incumbents, and the transitional effects were interpreted as an increased incumbency effect. Members are likely to have higher vote percentages and are much more likely to be safe when they are running in a district that is largely sympathetic to their party. When members run in districts less receptive to their party, fewer of them are likely to be safe. Over time the process of secular realignment created situations where many incumbents were running in districts supportive of the presidential candidate of the opposing party. Incumbents in districts won by the presidential candidate of the opposing party did not do as well as those in districts won by their presidential candidate. As incumbents in these conflicted (or *split-outcome*) districts retired and were replaced by candidates from the same party as that winning the presidential election, a higher percentage of incumbents did better, creating the appearance of a growing incumbency effect. Over time the partisan results in a greater percentage of House districts were coming in line with presidential results. The most significant changes have occurred for the Republican Party, and it is Republican incumbents who experienced an increase in safe seats during the 1960s.

The role of levels of presidential support in House districts for incumbents is indicated in Table 6.2. The presidential vote is used as an indicator of the relative partisan disposition of the district because it is the only candidacy presented to and eliciting a reaction from all districts. The table presents electoral support for incumbents, by party, by degree of support for their presidential candidates from 1900 to 2004. The results are divided by the party of the incumbent. This aggregation of results of 104 years, of course, conceals decades of change and how that change affected the electoral status of incumbents. Those changes and their effects for incumbents are crucial for this analysis. Nonetheless, establishing this simple relationship between presidential success and the fortunes of incumbents is the first step in understanding how change affects incumbents.

Several matters are important about the results. First, there is the distribution of incumbents by the vote percentages of their presidential candidates. Within each party, most incumbents have been in districts where their presidential candidate won at least 50 percent of the vote. Members of each party tend to win where their presidential candidate wins. Second, members win higher percentages of the vote when their presidential candidate does better. For Republican incumbents, their vote percentage and the percentage of members that are safe (60 percent or more) increase with the vote percentage of their presidential candidate. For Democratic incumbents the pattern is the same, except for those Democratic incumbents in districts where their presidential candidate won less than 40 percent of the vote. Incumbents in these districts won 66.9 percent of the vote.

Third, and most important for what follows, many House incumbents in both parties won in districts where their presidential candidate lost. These split outcomes increased during the transition in party bases and then declined as realignment played out. Eventually, it resulted in more safe Republican incumbents and created the appearance of an increase in the incumbency effect.

THE PATTERN OF CHANGE

Each party has experienced change in its electoral base, with presidential candidates generally doing better in so-called new areas before their House candidates do. The result is that the general relationship shown in Table 6.2 has varied over time. Figure 6.6 provides one indicator of how change has progressed. The figure tracks the correlation

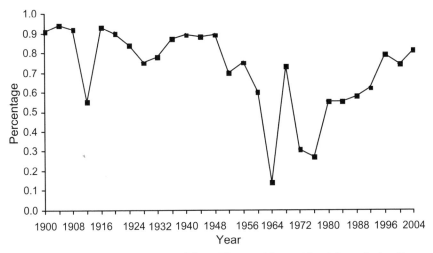

Figure 6.6. Correlation of Republican House with presidential results by district, 1900–2004. Includes all districts. Data compiled by the author.

between the percentage of the vote received by Republican presidential and House candidates for all districts since 1900.[3] That correlation was generally high from 1900 to 1944. Beginning in 1948, the Republican Party made some inroads into the South, but Democratic incumbents were able to continue to dominate southern elections for another 20–30 years. The result of the success of Republican presidential candidates in the South and the persistence of Democratic House members were the beginning of a declining national association between presidential and House results. During the 1960s and 1970s the relationship reached its lowest levels, indicating a distinct separation of the success of partisan presidential and House candidates. As incumbents retired and were replaced in many districts by candidates of the other party, the relationship began to return to its earlier levels. By 2004 that relationship had returned to a relatively high level.

[3] No data are available for the years 1900–1948 for presidential percentages by House district for those districts in the more populated counties. Some counties had more than one House district within its confines, and no one has acquired the presidential data by district within those counties to aggregate them by district. The number of such districts varies from 55 in 1900 to 125 in 1948. Afterward, presidential results are available by House district.

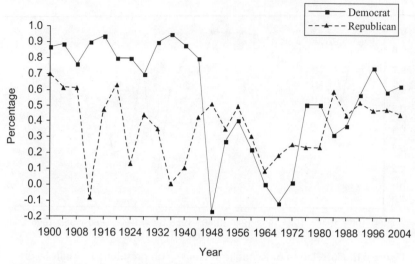

Figure 6.7. Correlation of Republican House with presidential results by party, 1900–2004. Includes all districts. Data compiled by the author.

This separation of presidential and House results has played out somewhat differently for the two parties. For Democrats the relationship began its decline in 1948, reflecting the demise of support for Democratic presidential candidates in the South. For Republicans the situation was different. Figure 6.7 focuses only on the correlation of incumbent with presidential results by party. From 1900 through 1944 the Republican correlation was never as high as that enjoyed by Democrats. It dropped even lower during the 1960s and 1970s, and only since the 1980s has it returned to the levels seen in the early part of the century. Even with this resurgence of the relationship, the Republican Party has struggled to bring presidential and House results together.

The changes in partisan presidential voting in House districts occurred faster than changes in partisan House votes because incumbents were able to stay in office and postpone the partisan transition of districts. The separation of presidential and House results put many incumbents in a situation where they were running in districts with a partisan disposition relatively unsympathetic to them. This increased the presence of split-outcome House districts, or those in which the partisan winner differs for the House and presidential races. Figure 6.8

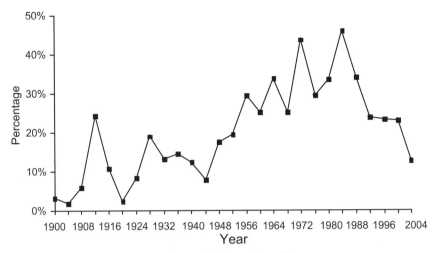

Figure 6.8. Percentage of House districts with split outcomes, 1900–2004.
See Appendix A. Data compiled by the author.

tracks the number of split-outcome House districts from 1900 to 2004.
From 1900 through the early 1950s, about 10 percent of House districts had split outcomes. That began to increase in 1956, and in
1984, 46 percent of districts had split outcomes. Their presence has
declined steadily since then as realignment has unfolded, and House
outcomes have come into line with presidential results (Stonecash,
2005: 67–88). In the 2004 elections the percentage of districts with
split outcomes had returned to 12.8, reaching a level not seen since
the 1940s.

The occurrence of split outcomes over time has not been similar for
the two parties, as shown in Figure 6.9. For both parties, split outcomes
were relatively infrequent from 1900 to 1928. The exceptions were
in 1912 for Republicans, when Teddy Roosevelt's run as a third-party
Progressive disrupted normal Republican voting patterns, and 1928,
when Democrats ran Al Smith, governor of New York. Smith fared
poorly in the South, and his support pattern differed considerably
from prior years.

Then, with the success of Franklin Roosevelt as the Democratic
presidential candidate from 1932 to 1944, many more Republican
incumbents found themselves running in districts won by Roosevelt.
Democrats had few split-outcome districts when the New Deal coalition

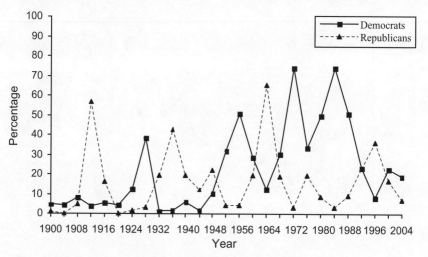

Figure 6.9. Percentage of House districts with split outcomes, 1900–2004, by party of incumbent. See Appendix A. Data compiled by the author.

was at its peak. Then, with Truman taking a stand on civil rights and Eisenhower following up on that by doing fairly well in the South, the tables turned, and many more Democrats found themselves running in districts where the Republican presidential candidate was winning the district. Most Democratic incumbents were able to hang on, resulting in a significant increase in split outcomes within that party.

For Republicans, despite their minority status within the House, they had far fewer split-outcome districts to contend with beginning in 1952. The candidacy of Goldwater in 1964 and the weak showing of Bob Dole as the Republican presidential candidate produced abrupt increases, but the match between House and presidential candidate results was clearly better for the party beginning in 1952. From 1952 to 2004 an average of 36.5 percent of Democratic incumbents had split outcomes in each presidential election year, while Republicans averaged 17.1 percent.

CONSEQUENCES

The evolution of this realignment had two consequences. First, it bene-fited Republican incumbents more than Democratic incumbents. The situation of Republican incumbents has improved, while Democratic incumbents have experienced little improvement. The next chapter will detail how the incumbents of each party have been affected.

Second, these changes created the impression that there was an increase in the incumbency effect and the retirement slump. The changes, however, should be seen more properly as reflective of transitions. With regard to the former, as incumbents who had been running against presidential results retired and were replaced by incumbents from the other party, the vote percentages of the new incumbents increased, resulting in greater incumbent electoral success. The new incumbent vote percentages rose because they were in districts more compatible to their partisanship and not because they were somehow capable of altering electoral margins. With regard to the retirement slump, as incumbents running against the presidential vote retired, the partisan vote in the district declined. That decline resulted in a significant retirement slump. The change, however, did not reflect the ability of the exiting incumbent to raise his or her vote percentage during a career; rather, it reflected the decline in the partisan vote when the incumbent exited. These two changes will be analyzed in the following chapters.

CHAPTER 7

A Partisan View of Incumbent Percentages

For much of the last century Republican incumbents were running in districts that were not strongly inclined to support their party. The process of realignment has gradually resulted in most now running in districts more amenable to them. That, in turn, has increased their electoral security. If that is occurring, we should be able to analyze incumbent election results by party and see changes largely benefiting Republican incumbents.

PARTY, AVERAGE VOTE PERCENTAGES, AND SAFE SEATS

The most frequently used indicator of the situation of an incumbent is the average vote percentage of the incumbent. The important matter is what happens when we examine this indicator from a partisan perspective. Prior analyses have examined all incumbents together. If only contested races are examined, there is an increase. If all incumbents are included, there is no increase after 1946. Indeed, as Figure 7.1 indicates, the only sustained increase in the vote percentages of all incumbents in the last century occurred in 1918, when the average of all incumbents increased from the lower 60s to the upper 60s. It has stayed at that level, with some fluctuations, since then. It is difficult to see any significant change from 1964 to 1966 in the overall average.

This average, while interesting, prevents us from seeing any changes that are partisan in nature. Figure 7.2 separates the average percentages of the vote won by incumbents by party. The major change over time is what has happened to Republicans. From 1900 through 1964 Republican incumbents always received a lower average percentage of

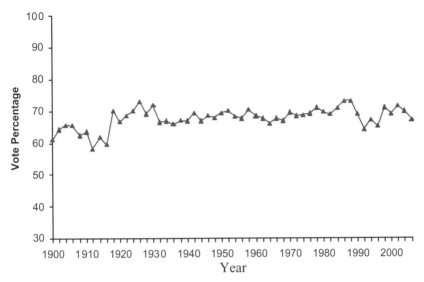

Figure 7.1. Average vote percentage for all House incumbents, 1900–2006. Data compiled by the author.

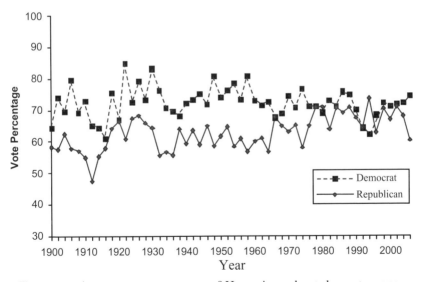

Figure 7.2. Average vote percentage of House incumbents by party, 1900–2006. Data compiled by the author.

the vote than Democrats. Much of this was due to Democratic dominance in the South, to be discussed later.

Something clearly happened in 1966, but only for Republicans. In
the five elections prior to 1966, the vote percentages of Republican
incumbents averaged 61.0 in 1956, 56.7 in 1958, 60.0 in 1960, 61.1
in 1962, and 56.6 in 1964. The average for those five elections was
59.1. Then, in 1966, their average vote jumped to 67.8. Democrats
had averaged 74.3 percent in the five prior elections, and in 1966,
their average percentage declined to 67.6. Democrats' average recov-
ered somewhat to 71.6 in 1968, but the Democratic decline and the
increase in the Republican average resulted in no net change in the
overall average. In 1980 the Republican average increased to about
70 and has remained at that level, with some minor fluctuations, since
then. The change in the vote percentages of incumbents in 1966
was partisan in nature.[1] Republicans experienced improved electoral
fortunes in 1966 and after, while Democrats were experiencing a very
gradual decline. It was not a change experienced by incumbents, but
by Republicans.

The increase in vote percentages in 1966 also affected the presence of safe seats, or those in which incumbents received more than
60 percent of the overall vote. The important matter is again the
1966 transition, as that is what Mayhew (1974a, 1974b) noticed.[2] Figure 7.3 presents the percentage of incumbents running who had safe
outcomes from 1946 to 2006. In 1966 and subsequent years, there was
an increase in the percentage of safe seats. Anyone comparing 1946–
1964 to 1966 and after would see a fairly significant shift in 1966. For

---

[1] This partisan change was not completely ignored. In a 1981 article, Melissa Collie
(1981: 125) noted that the increase in safe seats from 1964–1976 cohorts compared
to the 1952–1962 cohorts was much greater for Republicans than for Democrats.
She noted, "The partisan distribution of the marginal-to-safe pattern casts further
doubt on the uniformity of an increased incumbent advantage" (Collie, 1981: 125).
While the partisan nature of change was noted in her analysis, it was not pursued in
the analysis or in subsequent analyses.

[2] While the primary focus has been on the years since 1946, the work of Garand
and Gross suggests that there is an equally interesting long-term trend in the
presence of safe seats. The figure presents the percentage of all incumbents who
received 60 percent of the total vote from 1900 to 2006. The figure indicates the
importance of historical perspective. As Garand and Gross (1984) and Gross and
Garand (1984) have noted, there has been a fairly steady rise in the vote percentage and percentage of safe seats since the mid-1880s. What looks like a significant

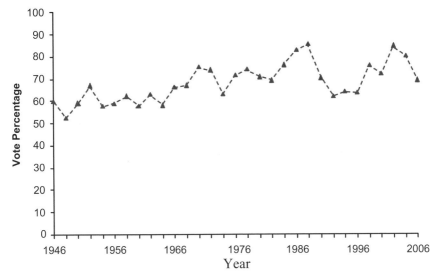

Figure 7.3. Percentage of House incumbents with 60 percent or more of the vote, 1946–2006. Data compiled by the author.

the five elections of 1956–1964 the average percentage of safe seats was 60.0, and for the years 1966–1974 the average was 69.1. It would be easy to conclude that incumbents *in general* were increasing their electoral security.

increase in 1966, if viewed in long-term perspective, looks less significant. Clearly some long-term changes are playing a role, and those changes are not just post-1946.

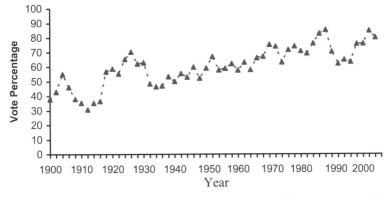

Percentage of House incumbents with 60 percent or more of the vote, 1900–2006. Data compiled by the author.

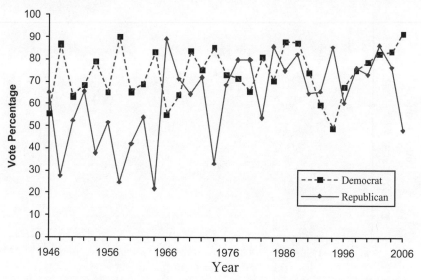

Figure 7.4. Percentage of House incumbents with 60 percent or more of the vote by party, 1946–2006. Data compiled by the author.

The difficulty is that the increase was not general, but was confined only to Republicans. Figure 7.4 presents the percentage of safe seats by party of the incumbent. From 1946 to 1964 Republicans always had fewer safe seats than Democrats. In 1966 Republicans experienced a surge in their percentage of safe seats from 21.6 to 89.2. Democrats experienced a decline, but the decline was not enough to offset the Republican surge. The overall percentage increased from 58.1 to 66.1, and the percentage for all incumbents remained higher after 1966, except for 2006. The source of the increase was because of changes experienced by Republicans, however, and not by all incumbents.

Furthermore, the increases experienced by the Republicans persisted. Table 7.1 expands on Table 5.1 and presents by party and era the percentage of the vote received by incumbents and the percentage of safe seats. The years 1946–1964 are presented separately to again provide an analysis in years comparable to the studies that focus on 1946 and after. From 1946 through 1964 Democrats had a significant advantage in the percentage of the vote received and the percentage of safe seats. Democrats averaged 14.6 percentage points more of the vote (74.8 to 60.2) than Republicans and had a 27 percentage point advantage in safe seats (70.9 to 43.6) over Republicans.

TABLE 7.1. *Electoral security of incumbents by era and party*

Region	Democrats			Republicans		
	N	% Vote	% Safe	N	% Vote	% Safe
1900–1930						
All	2,564	71.6	57.6	2,949	61.6	43.6
Non-South	1,212	57.5	27.5	2,854	61.0	43.6
South	1,352	84.3	84.6	95	63.1	45.3
1932–1944						
All	1,654	71.8	59.9	947	59.1	34.7
Non-South	1,034	61.2	40.8	929	59.0	34.3
South	620	89.4	91.6	18	65.2	55.6
1946–1964						
All	2,205	74.8	70.9	1,703	60.2	43.6
Non-South	1,245	64.1	55.7	1,634	60.1	44.3
South	960	88.6	90.7	69	63.0	42.0
1966–2006						
All	4,641	71.3	75.1	3,575	66.4	69.3
Non-South	3,272	69.0	73.5	2,642	64.5	67.5
South	1,369	76.6	78.8	933	71.8	74.5

*N*s refer to the number of elections in which an incumbent was present.

Source: Data compiled by the author.

Regionalism played a significant role in this party difference. Outside the South, Republican incumbents were only 4 percentage points below the Democratic average, but their average was only 60.1, or right at what has become defined as a safe seat. A majority of their seats fell below that mark. Democrats received a higher percentage of the vote (64.1), pushing 11 percent more of the Democratic seats into the safe category. Outside the South, the parties were not that far apart in their electoral success. The difference in the percentage of safe seats was largely because almost all Republican seats were outside the South and Democrats had a substantial percentage of their seats in the South, where almost all their seats were safe.

Two matters changed after 1964 for Republicans. More of the seats they held outside the South were in the safe category, and they also steadily acquired seats in the South, with most of them (74.5 percent) being safe. In contrast, during the post-1964 years, Democrats were experiencing a gradual erosion of their position. Overall, then, there was an increase in the percentage of safe House incumbents after 1964, but this increase was confined to Republican incumbents.

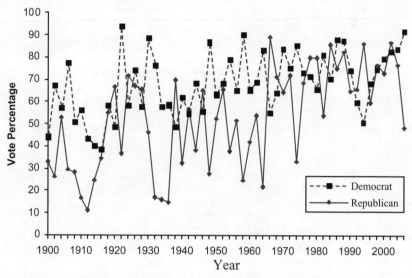

Figure 7.5. Percentage of House incumbents with 60 percent or more of the vote by party, 1900–2006. Data compiled by the author.

The important difference in regard to safe seats is that in the years 1946–2006 Republicans have been able to sustain their increase in the electoral security of incumbents. As Figure 7.5 indicates, Republican incumbents had occasionally matched the electoral security of Democratic incumbents in the years 1900–1964. They did match Democrats in terms of the percentage of safe seats in 1920, 1924, 1928, 1938, 1942, and 1946, but they would then slip badly the next year. After 1966 Republicans faced significant declines only in 1974 (Watergate), 1982 (a severe recession with Republican president Ronald Reagan), and 2006 (the negative reaction to Iraq and George Bush). They have generally quickly bounced back from these past setbacks. The important matter is, again, that the increase in the percentage of safe seats for incumbents beginning in 1966 was a partisan change, not a general increase.

CHANGES OVER THE CYCLES OF CAREERS

The change in the average percentage of the vote received by incumbents in the 1960s is a reflection of greater Republican success. Is

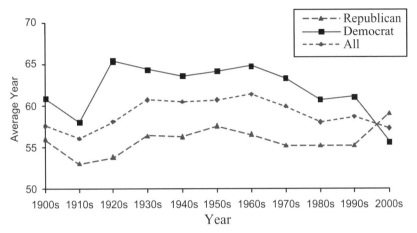

Figure 7.6. Average initial vote percentage for incumbents by decade of entry, 1900–2006.

an increase in their electoral fortunes evident when other indicators are examined? As was done earlier, it is possible to assess partisan differences for initial percentages, increases in vote percentages with successive years, and net changes over a career.

The first indicator involves changes in *initial* vote percentages for incumbents. Figure 7.6 presents the trend of initial percentages for all incumbents and by party over the last century. The average beginning percentage for all incumbents, despite a rise from the 1930s through the 1970s, is essentially at the same level now as in the early 1900s. The difference between the parties is that for almost the entire last century, Democratic incumbents have begun their careers with higher initial percentages. More Democrats have been safer from the beginning of their careers.

That difference between the parties in initial percentages was consistent until the 1960s, when the difference began to steadily diminish. In the 1960s Democrats began their careers with percentages that were 8.2 points higher than Republican percentages. Since then, differences have declined steadily, and for elections in the 2000s Republicans are now starting their careers with higher initial percentages than Democrats enjoy. While Republicans are now better off, the change has come about only lately, and the timing of the changes does not explain the change in Republican fortunes in the 1960s.

TABLE 7.2. *Ability to increase vote percentages by party and time groupings,*
1900–2006

Time period	N	Intercept	Initial %	No. of years	R^2
Democrats					
1900–1930	2,707	11.4	.82	.71	.63
1932–1944	2,014	13.6	.79	.45	.62
1946–1964	2,562	26.7	.63	.33	.46
1966–2006	5,303	37.2	.49	.18	.22
Republicans					
1900–1930	3,014	28.0	.50	.87	.24
1932–1944	1,161	39.9	.29	.09	.08
1946–1964	2,006	36.4	.37	.17	.12
1966–2006	4,125	37.2	.44	.36	.10

The Ns here refer to the number of elections involved. All members of the House who served just one term and chose not to run for reelection are excluded. A case is an election year and involves the independent variables of the initial percentage an incumbent received and the year of a legislator's career. The dependent variable is the vote percentage of a legislator in that year. If a legislator serves 10 years, the initial election is coded as 0 for year, and the fifth election is coded as 10 for the number of years in office. The analysis includes all members of the House elected in 1900 or after. Elections are grouped by the years of the election.

INCREASING THEIR VOTE PERCENTAGES
WITH YEARS IN OFFICE

If Republican incumbents have been doing better than Democrats in recent decades, perhaps the change is because their ability to increase their vote percentages with successive years in office has increased. The results presented earlier (Table 4.2) indicate that this ability for all incumbents has declined over time. Table 7.2 presents results by party, with election year results grouped as in Chapter 4. For the years 1900–1930, incumbents from both parties were relatively successful in increasing their vote percentages with successive years in office. Compared to later years, the relationship between years in office and vote percentages was relatively high for both parties. During these years Republicans were also more successful than Democrats in raising their vote percentages with successive years in office.

The interesting situations involve the years after 1944. The coefficient for Democrats continued to decline, reaching .18 for the years 1966–2006. For Republicans the opposite has occurred. Their

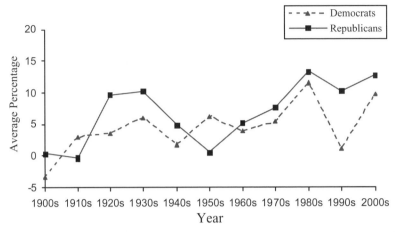

Figure 7.7. Average net change for incumbents by party and by decade of departure, 1900–2006. Data compiled by the author.

coefficient increased to .17 in 1946–1964 and then to .36 for 1966–2006. Over the last century Democratic incumbents have experienced a steady decline in their ability to improve their vote with time in office. Republicans, in contrast, have gradually rebounded from the 1930s and now have a coefficient twice as large as that of Democrats. Again, whatever improvement in the electoral fortunes of incumbents is occurring is not general in nature, but partisan. It is difficult to speak of an incumbency effect when the effects are confined to one party.

NET CAREER CHANGES

Greater Republican electoral success should also improve Republicans' ability to increase their vote percentages from the beginning to the end of their careers. Figure 7.7 presents average net changes by party, by decade over the last century. The relative ability of party incumbents to increase their vote fluctuated from 1900 through the 1950s. Since the 1960s, members of both parties have done fairly well in this regard, but Republican incumbents have consistently done better.

For every indicator of how well incumbents do – the average vote percentage received in each year by incumbents, the percentage of seats classified as safe, the initial vote percentage, the ability to increase that percentage once in office, and the net vote percentage increase over a career – Republicans have experienced an increase and Democrats have not. To portray these changes as reflective of some general increase in the incumbency effect misrepresents what has transpired in recent decades.

CHAPTER 8

The Role of Realignment

The major change regarding incumbents during the years 1946–2006 has been the growing electoral security of Republicans. Realignment and the gradual shift in the electoral bases of the parties are central to this change. As these shifts have occurred, led largely by changes in the electoral pursuits of presidential candidates, many incumbents have found themselves left behind by their parties. Republicans, in particular, have struggled with this, and many incumbents in the party have run in districts where their presidential candidates were not doing well, holding down their margin. Eventually, the party's out of synch incumbents retired and were replaced with incumbents in districts where Republican presidential candidates did well. These newer Republicans, running in districts more amenable to Republican ideas, won higher percentages, resulting in more safe Republicans.

The Republican changes have involved remarkable shifts in the electoral bases of their presidential candidates. In the early 1900s Republican presidential candidates did very well in New England and the remainder of the North[1] and poorly in the South. The aftermath of the Great Depression left them weakened in the first two areas and with very little support in the South. By the 2000s, Republican support has completely eroded in New England and is very strong in the South. The parties have essentially exchanged their areas of greatest strength over time (Stonecash, 2005); that is, what was strongly Democratic

---

[1] New England is defined here as Maine, New Hampshire, Vermont, Massachusetts, Rhode Island, and Connecticut. The North includes New York, New Jersey, Pennsylvania, Delaware, Maryland, Ohio, Michigan, Indiana, Illinois, Wisconsin, and Minnesota.

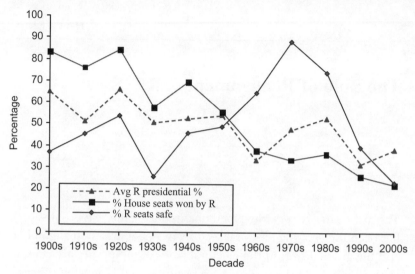

Figure 8.1. Republican success in presidential and House elections, New England, 1900–2006. Data compiled by the author.

has become strongly Republican, and what was strongly Republican is now strongly Democratic.

The sequence of changes within regions is important. Presidential election results began to shift with House results lagging because incumbents could ward off the change for a while. Incumbency mattered in that a sitting House member could exploit his or her visibility to survive as change was occurring. Eventually, incumbents were either defeated or retired, and House results caught up with presidential results. To track these changes, the analysis will first focus on the two extremes (New England and the South) and then review the remainder of the nation. The Republican Party had a different experience in each of these regions.

NEW ENGLAND

Figure 8.1 indicates how the situation of Republicans changed in New England over time. If Republican presidential votes are taken as a sign of party support, in the early 1900s, the party did well. That success carried many Republican House candidates to success, and Republicans won over 60 percent of seats in the region through the 1950s.

As support for the Republican Party and presidential success gradually eroded, the success of all Republican candidates declined.

The effect of this drop was a temporary and deceiving effect on the percentage of safe Republican incumbent outcomes within the region. With presidential support dropping, fewer new Republicans were getting elected, and fewer incumbents were surviving. From the 1950s through the 2000s the number of incumbents running in elections (all years during each decade) declined from 74 in the 1950s to 42 in the 1960s, 34 in the 1970s, 38 in the 1980s, 23 in the 1990s, and 13 in the 2000s. The party was gradually losing incumbents in this region, with marginal members more likely to disappear, leaving only members with relatively strong support.

In the transition years of the 1960s–1980s the elimination of more vulnerable members resulted in an apparent rise in the percentage of safe incumbents, but it was really that those left were in a stronger situation. The changes from 1964 to 1966 are indicative. In 1964, 10 Republican incumbents ran for reelection in this region. Two of the 10 lost, and another 2 received 50.1 and 63.0 percent, respectively. These latter two then retired in 1966. The four who departed averaged 52.5 percent in 1964. In contrast, the six who survived in 1964 and ran again in 1966 averaged 65.4 percent in 1964 and 71.3 percent in 1966. The party then picked up two more seats in the 1966 surge toward Republicans across the country, and the average percentage of the vote won by the eight Republican incumbents running in 1968 was 73.8. Every incumbent running in 1968 had a percentage above 60, and all were safe. The party lost a net of two seats as a result of the 1964–1966 elections, but those remaining were safer. The party was gradually losing electoral support, but those remaining were better off. The party was shrinking to its safest electoral base over time. The appearance of an increase in incumbent electoral security was also a decline for the party. After the 1970s, there were few districts in New England where a Republican incumbent ran and a Republican presidential candidate received more than 60 percent of the vote. The decline of the party has continued, and after the 2006 elections, only one Republican incumbent remained, and that individual was not safe.[2]

---

[2] That individual was Christopher Shays from Connecticut.

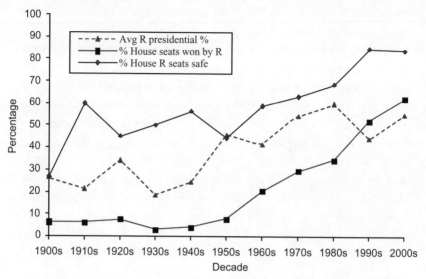

Figure 8.2. Republican success in presidential and House elections, South, 1900–2006. Data compiled by the author.

THE SOUTH

In stark contrast with New England, beginning in the 1950s, Republicans in the South began to experience growing success (Figure 8.2). Republican presidential candidates increased their average vote percentages to the mid-40s in the 1950s and 1960s, and the percentage has gradually increased since then. Success in House elections began to increase in the 1960s and has steadily risen since then.

Those incumbents winning elections were also safe. While the party had only a few seats in the first half of the century, the seats it was winning were relatively safe. Beginning in the 1960s, Republicans began to win more seats, and more of them were safe. In the years 1966–2006, 89 percent of Republican incumbents were running in districts won by Republican presidential candidates. The result was that almost all Republican incumbents were safe. Realignment brought the party greater success for its presidential and House candidates, and the overlap in party success created the basis for a significant increase in the presence of Republican safe seats in this region.

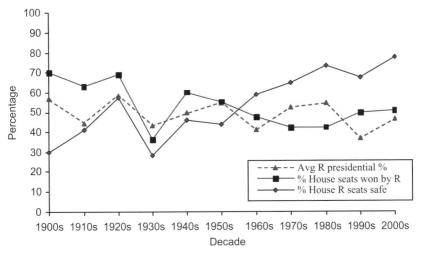

Figure 8.3. Republican success in presidential and House elections, remainder of nation, 1900–2006. Data compiled by the author.

THE REMAINDER

While the Republican Party has gradually lost almost all of its incumbents in New England and gained a considerable number in the South, the party has had a more volatile experience in the remaining states. The party's percentage of the presidential vote and its percentage of seats won have fluctuated roughly around 50 percent over time, as shown in Figure 8.3. While presidential success has not changed, the party fared better in terms of safe seats for its incumbents. In the 1960s the percentage of Republican incumbents with safe seats began to steadily increase.

The important question is how Republicans could have had more safe seats even though their overall electoral security in the remainder of the nation was not increasing. The answer is that the lengthy realignment occurring was resulting in more Republican incumbents running in districts that were also being won by its presidential candidates. Table 8.1 indicates the changes the party was experiencing in all states. The first column indicates the success of Republican presidential candidates across all House districts. From 1900 to 1930 the

TABLE 8.1. *The shifting success of Republican incumbents, remainder of the nation, 1900–2004*[3]

| | | | % Republican incumbents | |
| | % All house districts won by Rep. presidential candidates | *N* | In districts won by Rep. presidential candidates | % of Republican incumbents safe in districts won by Rep. presidential candidates |
Years				
1900–1930	73.8	1,623	88.5	49.6
1932–1944	36.6	794	57.4	39.1
1946–1964	54.9	1,358	70.1	51.5
1966–2004	59.7	2,877	83.8	77.7

party's presidential candidates won 73.8 percent of all House districts. The emergence of the New Deal coalition vastly diminished the party's success, and from 1932 to 1944 Republican presidential candidates won only 36.6 percent of all House districts. Since 1946, they have fared better, winning over 50 percent of House districts.

The crucial matter is how the overlap of success in presidential and House elections changed over time. That overlap was high in 1900–1930 and then declined in 1932–1944. During 1900–1930, 88.5 percent of Republican incumbents were running in districts won by Republican presidential candidates. Then, during 1932–1944, only 57.5 percent of Republican incumbents were running in districts won by Republican candidates. Even those incumbents running in districts won by a Republican presidential candidate did not do particularly well, with only 39.1 percent of these incumbents falling into the safe category.

As party presidential success increased after 1964, two changes occurred that resulted in more safe Republican incumbents in these states. As realignment evolved, more House Republican candidates were running in districts also won by their presidential candidates.

---

[3] This analysis is done for all House districts for which there are presidential results. For the years 1900–1948, there were a growing number of multiple districts within a single county for which we do not have presidential results by county. These are districts for which the results have never been broken down within the county by House district. This number grows over time, as more of the population becomes located in large urban counties such as New York, Boston, Philadelphia, and Cook County (Chicago).

Fewer incumbents were running in districts won by the other party's presidential candidates. For 1966–2006 the percentage of Republican incumbents running in districts won by their presidential candidates increased to 83.8. In this latter time period, Republicans also experienced an increase in the percentage of safe incumbents among those who were running in districts won by their presidential candidates. They were increasingly able to capitalize on a more sympathetic electoral base to build larger margins of victory.

Republican incumbents struggled for years to achieve vote percentages equivalent to the percentages enjoyed by Democratic incumbents. They were finally able to achieve parity in 1966–2006, resulting in a significant increase in the percentage of their seats that were safe. For 1900–1930, for the entire nation, the average Republican incumbent won 57.4 percent of the vote. That percentage increased to 58.9 in 1932–1944, to 60.0 in 1946–1964, and then increased substantially to 65.4 in 1966–2006. The increase in the latter years pushed many more Republican incumbents into the category of being a safe seat. More incumbents were running in districts being won by Republican presidential candidates, which resulted in more safe incumbent Republican seats.

A SUMMARY

Realignment change has played out differently across the nation for Republicans. In New England the party has steadily lost support, and despite the relatively brief survival of some safe House incumbents, they eventually disappeared, leaving the party with only one unsafe incumbent by 2006. While the party was losing support in that region, its support was steadily growing in the South, and almost all its incumbents there were in districts won by Republican presidential candidates, and almost all were safe. In the remainder of the nation, there was a gradual re-sorting, with more and more incumbents running in districts being won by their presidential candidates. With more incumbents running in hospitable districts, the party was able to increase its percentage of safe members.

These changes are summarized for the entire nation in Table 8.2. For 1900–1930, 88.5 percent of Republican incumbents were in

TABLE 8.2. *Electoral conditions of House incumbents over time, the nation, by party, 1900–2006*

	Years			
	1900–1930	1932–1944	1946–1964	1966–2006
Republican incumbents				
% in 60%+ pres. districts	58.8	16.4	38.6	43.4
% safe	70.0	85.1	75.2	86.5
% in 50%+ pres. districts	88.5	57.7	70.4	84.1
% safe	50.7	40.6	52.9	78.7
% in <50% pres. districts	11.5	42.3	29.6	15.9
% safe	11.2	12.6	18.2	43.9
Democratic incumbents				
% in 60%+ pres. districts	55.8	68.7	41.6	28.5
% safe	85.3	93.2	94.2	91.6
% in 50%+ pres. districts	80.5	95.8	67.8	57.1
% safe	64.3	71.9	85.3	82.1
% in <50% pres. districts	19.5	4.2	32.2	42.9
% safe	15.2	7.4	47.3	60.4

districts won by their presidential candidates, and 58.8 percent of their incumbents were in districts in which their presidential candidates won 60 percent or more. The fortunes of the Republican Party plummeted in 1932–1944, with only 16.4 percent of its incumbents in districts won by 60 percent or more by its presidential candidates. In 1946–1964 the party's ability to have incumbents running in districts won by their presidential candidates increased, and in 1966–2006 it increased even further. Furthermore, the ability of Republican incumbents to do well in districts where the Republican presidential candidate won increased over time. The party had more incumbents running in such districts, and the percentage of incumbents in that situation who were safe steadily increased over time. The increase in the percentage of safe Republican incumbents that occurred in 1966 and after was due to increasingly large numbers of incumbents running in districts hospitable to them. Much of the incumbency effect literature has appeared to presume that the rise of incumbent success is general in nature and largely just a reflection of the resources and actions of incumbents, somehow independent of their electoral context. Quite the contrary, more incumbents are running in favorable electoral contexts, and that has increased the presence of safe seats.

The partisan nature of change is also evident in the Democratic situation. In the early part of the century the party had 80.5 percent of its incumbents in districts won by its presidential candidates. This percentage increased in the years 1932–1944, when the New Deal coalition was dominant. During those years, 95.8 percent of Democratic House members were running in districts in which their presidential candidates won. To return to Figure 6.9, which details the rise of split outcomes by party, House and presidential outcomes matched up, and the party had few split outcomes.

Then Republican presidential candidates began to make inroads into districts held by Democratic House members, and the presence of split outcomes increased dramatically in the 1950s. That increase persisted through the 1980s, and then declined rapidly in the 1990s, as Democrats either retired or were defeated and Republicans took seats previously held by Democrats. The result was that more Republican incumbents were running in districts that their presidential candidates were winning. For the years 1966–2004, 84.1 percent of Republican incumbents were in this situation, a level not experienced since the early 1900s.

The process that brings about this alignment of the sentiment of districts (measured here by presidential results) with House outcomes is both gradual and shaped by very specific events. House incumbents survive for years in hostile districts and eventually leave for a variety of reasons. Some are older and just decide to retire for age or health reasons. Some read the national mood, see it as unreceptive to their party, and decide that the strategic move is to retire (Jacobson, 2001: 153–60). In 1994, a bad year for Democrats, 10.6 percent of all seats were open because incumbents retired. Of the 46 open seats, 32 of 46 were vacated by Democrats. Others approach the reapportionment that occurs every 10 years and, after reviewing their new district and the need to cope with a substantially new constituency, decide to retire. For the last 20 years the percentage of open seats has generally been less than 10 percent. Reapportioned districts take effect every 10 years in years ending in 02. In the years following reapportionment, the percentage of open seats was higher. In 1992 it was 20.5 percent, and in 2002 it was 11.3 percent. All these retirement decisions, whether due to age and health, to reapportionment, or to the national mood, remove incumbents. That creates the possibility that these districts, if the House outcomes are out of line, will have partisan House outcomes congruent with presidential outcomes.

National vote swings also change the outcome in many districts that might have been split. Periodically – 1964, 1966, 1974, 1994, 2006 – substantial numbers of incumbents lose. Many of these outcomes create a split outcome where none existed, but others eliminate split outcomes and create more seats in which an incumbent is relatively safe.

This process of change is by no means over. Democrats still have more House seats in districts won by Republican presidential candidates than Republicans have House seats won by Democratic presidential candidates. After the 2006 elections, there were 58 Democrats in districts won by Bush in 2004 and 9 Republicans in districts won by Kerry. Change will continue, and it appears that the prospects of increased Republican success are good.

THE 1964–1966 SHIFT: WHAT HAPPENED?

The long-term story here is that Republicans have improved their fortunes by having more incumbents in districts favorable to their success. That changed a party with relatively few safe incumbents into one with far more in that category. There is still, however, the question of what happened in 1966. Why did a party with 43.6 percent of its incumbents safe during 1946–1964 suddenly have 83 percent of its incumbents in that category in 1966, and why did that continue?

There are at least two possible explanations, only one of which is supported by data. The 1964 election, which cost the party numerous incumbents, might have eliminated many marginal incumbents who were running in districts won by Democratic presidential candidates. The result may have been that the party was left with relatively stronger candidates. The new winners in 1966 might have won in districts inclined to elect Republicans, and these new candidates may have been more likely to be safe. The election may have shifted the party's electoral base from districts relatively inhospitable to those more sympathetic to Republicans. The alternative is that there may have been a general, across-the-board increase in support for Republican incumbents.

TABLE 8.3. *Percentage of Republican incumbents who were safe by year of election and district situation*

	Year of election							
	1962		1964		1966		1968	
	N	%	N	%	N	%	N	%
Region								
North	102	52.0	109	19.3	86	87.2	104	76.9
South	7	71.4	11	27.3	17	82.4	27	44.4
Other	46	56.5	51	25.5	36	94.4	49	75.5
Percent nonwhite								
0–9	144	54.9	156	22.4	121	89.3	150	77.3
10–19	10	50.0	13	15.4	8	87.5	14	57.1
20–29	1	.0	2	.0	4	100.0	8	50.0
30+	0	.0	0	.0	6	66.7	8	12.5
Median family income								
Lower	32	46.9	35	14.3	37	94.6	54	55.6
Middle	48	52.1	57	15.8	39	94.9	50	78.0
Higher	75	58.7	79	29.1	63	81.0	76	79.0
Republican presidential vote average, 1964 and 1968								
<40	35	45.8	34	29.4	24	70.9	34	67.7
40–49	94	51.1	110	17.3	78	91.0	109	68.8
50–59	24	75.0	25	24.0	35	94.3	35	82.9
60+	2	100.0	2	100.0	2	100.0	2	100.0

The data, shown in Table 8.3, do not support the first alternative. It is not the case that the degree of Republican success shifted from 1964 to 1966 and 1968 by type of district. If the success of Republican incumbents is compared across 1962–1968 by region, income, percentage of nonwhites, or the average vote for Republican presidential candidates, there is no clear change in their relative success by district type. The party did not increase its percentage of safe seats just in mostly white districts or in districts that voted strongly for Republican presidential candidates. There was a relatively greater increase in safe seats in middle- and higher-income districts, and that might reflect a movement of the party to appeal to higher-income voters (Stonecash and Lindstrom, 1999).

But the overall pattern seems to fit an alternative explanation better. That alternative is that there was a general increase in support for the party. The short-term evidence of 1962–1968 and the accumulated

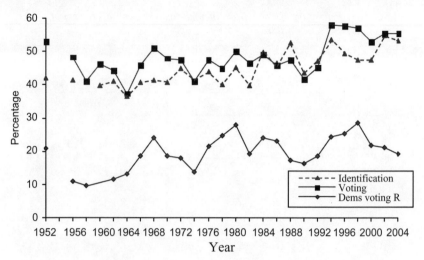

Figure 8.4. Percentage identifying as Republican, percentage voting Republican in House elections, and percentage of Democrats voting Republican, 1952–2006. Data from NES 1948–2004 cumulative file.

evidence since then support that argument. The evidence in Table 8.3 suggests that the presence of safe seats increased in all types of districts, not just ones we might think would be more supportive of Republicans. In almost every category (except the South, where the number of seats increased), there was a higher percentage of safe seats in 1968 compared to 1962.

The long-term evidence indicates that 1966 was the beginning of an improvement in the party's fortunes. Figure 8.4 tracks three indicators of individual-level partisan behavior: the percentage of those voting in House elections who identify themselves as Republican, the percentage of voters supporting Republican House candidates, and the percentage of voters identifying themselves as Democratic but voting for Republican House candidates. Identification with the Republican Party does not increase significantly in 1966 over the average of prior years, but there is a relatively substantial increase in the percentage of all voters voting Republican and of Democratic identifiers voting Republican.

If the years 1952–1964 are compared to 1966–2006, there is clear evidence that Republican fortunes improved beginning in 1966. Among those voters voting in House elections, the average percentage identifying themselves as Republican increased from 40.4 to 46.2. The percentage of those voters voting for House Republican candidates rose from 45.0 to 49.5. The percentage of those voters identifying themselves as Democrats but voting for House Republican candidates increased from 13.2 to 21.3. Finally, the percentage point advantage that the Democratic Party had over Republicans in party identification (not shown) declined from −19.0 to −5.2. The increase in the Republican incumbent average vote percentage and in the percentage of their incumbent seats that were safe seats increased and stayed higher because of a sustained movement toward Republicans (Jacobson, 2000b).

Why this shift occurred in 1966 is not entirely clear. Some argue that the liberal legislation of the Great Society under President Lyndon Johnson provoked a counterreaction, pushing the country in a more conservative direction (Stimson, 2005). The party gained seats in the South from 1962 to 1968 and pursued a strategy to attract more conservatives (Phillips, 1969). It is very possible that the combination of short-term reactions to national events in 1965–1966 and the party's beginning pursuit of a more conservative direction changed the fortunes of Republican incumbents, but not that of Democratic incumbents (Brewer and Stonecash, 2009).

Regardless, the evidence indicates that the important change in recent decades has been the improvement in the fortunes of Republican incumbents. Why that improvement occurred deserves much, much more analysis than is possible here. But it is clear that the fortunes of all incumbents did not improve.

CHAPTER 9

Conclusions and Implications

In the 1970s a consensus began to develop that House incumbents, all incumbents, were becoming safer. Given the context of American politics at that time – declining partisanship, increased ticket split-ting, more office resources for members – it seemed plausible that incumbents were able to create more of a personal vote. It was a reasonable proposition that incumbents were able to increase their visibility and that more voters could be coaxed to support visible candidates, making it more difficult for challengers to do well versus incumbents.

The evidence, however, suggests there is much to doubt about whether the House has witnessed an increase in the incumbency effect. If there has been a change, it is in the ability of House Republicans to increase their vote percentages and achieve the status of being safe. There has been a significant partisan realignment in American politics that has put many more Republican incumbents in districts that their presidential candidates won. More Republican incumbents are running in districts amenable to Republican appeals, and that made increasing their incumbent vote percentages easier.

Evaluating and accepting this alternative interpretation will take some time. There will be critiques and counteranalyses. How we finally interpret the time period of the 1950s through now will not be resolved for some time. This analysis is essentially a first effort to present an alternative way of seeing the changes of recent decades, and there is much more to explore about how these changes have played out over time. While there is much to pursue, the broad outlines of change are clear. Democrats have experienced little gain in recent decades, while Republicans have.

THE NORMATIVE ISSUE

The larger issue is how we see elections. While the immediate issue is empirical – what is happening to incumbent vote percentages over time – this issue emerged accompanied by a significant normative focus. The consensus that incumbents were doing better led to arguments about the need for term limits, unease about how officeholders were exploiting public resources, and concern that incumbents had too great an advantage in access to campaign finance funds. The broader concern was that these changes might be reducing the responsiveness of House members to public opinion. There seemed to be much to worry about regarding the democratic process.

This normative concern was first evident in Mayhew's (1974b) work. His seemingly simple view of members of Congress was that they were interested in being reelected. What was new was that he posited this single-minded objective as a simple way to organize how we see politicians' activities (Bond, 2001; Dodd, 2001). To achieve this, they engaged in position taking, credit claiming, and advertising. They sought to announce policy positions, claimed they had done something to help their constituents, and sought to inform the electorate about who they were and what they had done.

The argument was that members of Congress were using the greater resources of office to manipulate their image before the electorate and increase their chances of reelection. Mayhew (1974a: 304–13) and Fiorina (1977a, 1977b: 56–70) documented the growth of official resources of office and suggested that these resources (district mailings, constituency service, and local grants, or so-called pork) were giving incumbents a greater advantage in elections. If these resources were not enough, incumbents were also able to outspend challengers by large amounts (Jacobson, 1978). There was an implicit sense that perhaps politicians were doing too much for the public and were somehow too responsive to voters (Hurley, 2001: 260). The normative overtones were sometimes muted, but Fiorina (1977b), in discussing whether contemporary legislators have become more concerned with reelection, suggests they are not, but then notes that members of Congress, with all their resources, could

> deemphasize controversial policy positions and instead place heavy emphasis on nonpartisan, nonprogrammatic constituency service. . . . We do not need to postulate a congressman who is more interested in reelection today than previously. All we need postulate is a congressman sufficiently interested in reelection that he would rather be reelected as an errand boy than not reelected at all. (p. 37)

In other words, politicians could curry the favor of individual constituents by being responsive in providing particularistic help, while neglecting the larger issues, insulating themselves from controversy (Burnham, 1975). The result was that problems were avoided and voters were alienated from politics (Fiorina, 1980). Incumbents might have tried to look like they were doing something by claiming credit, but the suggestion was that they really were not focused on actually dealing with major issues and getting anything done. While politicians might have been happy with these developments, the democratic system was being harmed. Academics did not see these greater resources for politicians as a positive:

> Members of Congress have also given themselves an astonishing array of official resources that can be used to pursue reelection. These include salary, travel, office, staff and communication allowances. (Jacobson, 1983: 31)

It is hard to miss the negative normative overtone when salary, an office, staff, and the means to communicate are regarded as "astonishing."

The impact of these works was reflected in the kinds of research that emerged in subsequent years. The focus became how electoral outcomes were a product of members exploiting the advantages of office. The primary concern became how official resources, campaign spending, and reapportionment were increasing the incumbency effect and reducing electoral competitiveness. The information gathered – frequency of trips home, number of mailings, size of office staffs, number of press releases, and campaign spending – reflects preoccupation with the issue of how members exploit public resources to reduce competition.

The motivating concern was an anxiety about representation. Do politicians have too many resources to curry the favor of constituents? Are they too concerned with providing benefits to constituents, such that members are distracted from focusing on the larger (public interest) issues? The concerns seemed almost a throwback to the Progressives and their concern that incumbents were more concerned with reelection than representation (Hofstadter, 1955). How much are politicians exploiting office to help themselves and not necessarily democracy? As Hurley (2001) notes, in assessing the impact of *The Electoral Connection,*

> the book may easily be read as an indictment of electorally- or constituency-motivated behavior on charges of producing bad public policy. In some respects, then, the indictment of the electoral connection is an indictment of democracy. . . . The normative implications of a critique of Congress that faults the institution for being too representative are disturbing. (p. 260)

The focus on member resources and activities meant that district constituencies largely disappeared from these studies. By the early 1990s, it was impossible to find any congressional texts or studies that even contained a table presenting demographic variations in districts and a cross-tabulation of those district traits (income, density, race composition) with partisan outcomes. The central concern had become how much candidates, and primarily incumbents, can affect electoral outcomes using resources they control. While incorporating district population traits had been common in earlier works (Turner, 1951; MacRae, 1952; Cummings, 1966; Mayhew, 1966; Turner and Schneier, 1970), the focus on members and their resources eliminated that focus. The result was that the essence of partisan politics – connections among electoral policy concerns, party stances, and electoral responses – was seen as declining.

The results of the analysis in this book suggest that partisan electoral inclinations within districts have been of central importance. Republicans sought to deal with their minority status by appealing to new electorates. That eventually changed their policy goals and their constituency and prompted an enormous change in electoral align-ments. Democrats sought to expand their electoral base in the North, and their efforts subsequently changed their electoral base. Politics about policy issues was at work, and not the politics of avoiding issues. Parties were seeking new constituencies and found them, and that created change.

While the academic community was developing studies suggesting that representation was somehow being manipulated and perhaps diminished, the parties were engaged in a process of trying to find, represent, and attract constituents. The normative implications and concerns that emerged from the incumbency effect literature appear to have been misplaced.

We may have much less to worry about than some researchers have suggested regarding American elections involving incumbents. There is no doubt that incumbents have an advantage in elections. That has been the case from the beginning of the nation, and we should all be surprised if a House member who has been in office for two or more years does not have an advantage over someone probably less well known. There is an incumbency advantage, which is why most incumbents within any given year win. The issue is whether that advantage is increasing and somehow putting incumbents in situa-tions where they can pay less attention to voters. This analysis provides little evidence for the argument that their advantage is increasing. It also suggests that some of the concern about representation may need to be reconsidered.

PART III

Appendices:
More Detailed Analyses of Incumbency
Effect Indicators

Realignment and the Retirement Slump: A Closer Look

The presumed rise in the incumbency effect in recent decades was really the emergence of greater electoral success for Republican incumbents. While that evidence is clear, there is one further indicator to consider in greater detail. The retirement slump indicator has a clear trend over the last century, with higher scores recorded in the second half of the century. While the problems with this indicator were discussed earlier – the indicator also reflects changes from open-seat to open-seat contests – the trend of the indicator is still likely to be cited by some as an indication that incumbents are doing better.

Not only does the indicator rise over time, but the rise is essentially the same for both parties. Figure A.1 shows the average for all existing incumbents along with the results separated by party. The trend is clearly upward over time. The issue is why, if there has not really been a significant change in incumbent fortunes.

While the rise is in part a product of the greater shift from open-seat to open-seat outcomes, discussed in Chapter 5, there has also been a clear change in outcomes after an incumbent leaves. Figure A.2 repeats from prior analyses the average change in partisan votes after incumbents left office by year for 1904–2006. The results are presented in terms of Democratic percentages, so the differences in shift by the party of the incumbent can be tracked. When a Republican incumbent leaves, the Democratic vote percentage generally increases, meaning there is a drop in the Republican percentage. When a Democratic incumbent leaves, the votes generally become less Democratic, or a drop in the partisan vote occurs.

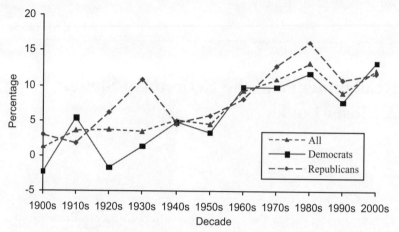

Figure A.1. Average retirement slump for incumbents by party and by decade of departure, 1900–2006. Data compiled by the author.

The important matter is the trend of changes over time. For the first 50 years, the changes after an incumbent left fluctuated around zero, or no change, and the only apparent difference between the parties was that changes following Democrats seemed to fluctuate more than was the case for Republicans. Then, in the 1960s, the change from the last election of an incumbent to the open seat increased for each party. The changes were clearly bigger.

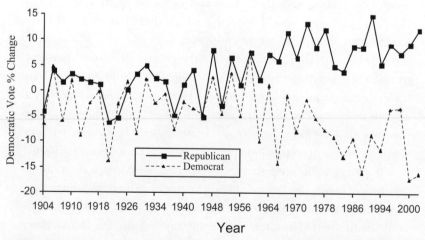

Figure A.2. Democratic vote changes in open seats by prior party winner, 1904–2004.

Something changed in the 1960s, and the greater changes that began then could certainly be looked at as reflecting a greater retirement slump. The question to be addressed is whether these changes might be explained as reflecting something else. Might they be a reflection of the changes accompanying realignment?

REALIGNMENT AND PARTISAN SHIFTS

The presumed value of the retirement slump indicator is that it captures how much an incumbent has been able to temporarily increase the partisan vote in a district. The calculation is based on the assumption that the partisan vote generally returns to the level that prevailed when the exiting incumbent first ran for office. There may be random fluctuations from one open-seat race to the next, but the logic of using this indicator appears to be the assumption of a relatively stable set of partisan inclinations in districts over time. This stability makes calculating the drop in the partisan vote from the incumbent to the level realized by the open-seat candidate mean something.

The difficulty, as discussed in Chapter 5, is that both the career increase in the vote achieved by the incumbent and the change in the partisan vote from the prior open seat affect the derived retirement slump score. If open-seat to open-seat changes did not occur, the derived score would be a valid indicator. An initial percentage of 55, followed by an eventual level of 65 for an incumbent in the last election and 55 in the next election, would yield a retirement slump of 10. The difficulty is that there is remarkable movement from one open seat to another, significantly affecting the resulting retirement scores. The combined effect of career changes and open-seat to open-seat changes complicates the calculation, as discussed in Chapter 5.

While the open-seat to open-seat changes are a complication, they are not just random fluctuations that somehow distort matters. They may also reflect something else occurring. Net career changes (what the incumbent achieves or does not achieve) and open-seat to open-seat changes (partisan tendencies in the district) are related, and their relationship reflects the impact of realignment. The remainder of this appendix presents another way to think about changes involving incumbents and then presents an analysis of changes using that framework.

As noted in Chapter 8, there has been a long-term realignment in American politics. Regions of the country that were once Republican have moved to support Democrats, and regions that supported Democrats have moved to support Republicans. This process of change creates another way to think about net career changes and open-seat to open-seat changes. If districts are gradually shifting in their voting allegiance, then that should produce some clear patterns of partisan change. Districts that are moving *toward* one party should have consistent signs that the partisan vote is moving toward the party. Districts that are moving *away* from a party should have consistent signs that the partisan vote is moving away from the party. There is not just random variation occurring.

If realignment is washing over House districts, incumbents moving toward a party should show positive net career gains and the districts they held should show positive open-seat to open-seat partisan changes. The presidential vote should also be moving their way, reflecting the underlying partisan shift. Incumbents in districts moving away from a party should show net negative career gains and negative open-seat to open-seat partisan changes. The presidential vote should also be moving away from the party. In other words, net career changes and open-seat to open-seat changes should be correlated, since both are reflections of the shift of the district toward a party. Incumbents running in districts shifting toward them should do well, while those running in districts moving away from them should struggle to maintain support in the district. The relationship between net career changes and open-seat to open-seat changes is not just a complication in the calculation of this indicator. They may well be systematically related.

Figure A.3 indicates the relationship between net career changes (increase or decrease in incumbent vote percentages from the initial to the last election) and open-seat to open-seat partisan changes for all exiting incumbents from 1900 to 2006. For career changes, a positive number means the incumbent's vote percentage increased over the course of his or her career, while a negative number means it decreased. For open-seat to open-seat changes, a positive number

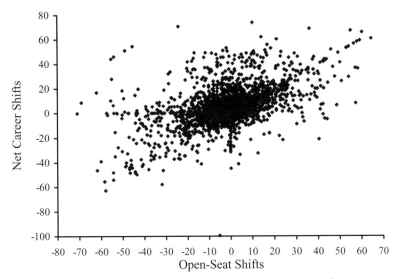

Figure A.3. Net career changes and open-seat shifts, 1900–2006.

means the vote for the party of the incumbent increased from the first time he or she ran until the vote for the next candidate of the same party ran in an open seat. There is a large percentage of cases that cluster in the middle, but the scatterplot does not represent a pattern of random association. There is a positive relationship between career changes and open-seat to open-seat changes. The bivariate correlation between the two is .49.

The pattern fits what we would expect if systematic change is occurring. Incumbents do better in districts moving toward their party (as measured by the open-seat to open-seat change) and worse in districts that are moving away from their party. It does not appear that open-seat to open-seat changes are just random fluctuations that complicate the calculation of the retirement slump. These open-seat changes are reflections of systematic partisan shifts away or toward a specific party.

A primary concern of this analysis is why the retirement slump increased beginning in the 1960s. The relationship shown in Figure A.3 is important in understanding the retirement slump and changes in it for two reasons. First, it indicates just how limited the indicator is as a reflection of changes involving incumbents. Second, analyzing that first matter helps us isolate and understand why the retirement slump increased.

TABLE A.1. *Retiring House member changes, 1900–1958 and 1960–2006*

	Career Δ +/ Open Δ −	Career Δ −/ Open Δ −	Career Δ +/ Open Δ +	Career Δ −/ Open Δ +
1900–1958				
No. of cases	276	342	475	106
% all cases	23.0	28.5	39.6	8.8
Beginning House %	58.7	69.1	59.2	64.4
Ending House %	67.4	58.8	72.5	58.9
Career change	8.7	−10.2	13.3	−5.5
Next open seat %	50.3	54.9	71.5	71.1
Open-seat change	−8.5	−14.1	12.2	6.7
Retirement slump	16.9	3.9	1.0	−12.3
Beginning presidential %	57.4	63.2	62.1	65.3
Ending presidential %	57.7	55.9	63.2	59.6
1960–2006				
No. of cases	378	249	371	51
% all cases	36.0	23.7	35.4	4.9
Beginning House %	58.4	70.5	54.9	66.0
Ending House %	70.6	60.0	72.2	56.7
Career change	12.2	−10.7	17.3	−9.3
Next open seat %	47.3	53.0	67.5	74.0
Open-seat change	−11.1	−17.5	12.6	8.0
Retirement slump	23.1	7.0	4.7	−17.3
Beginning presidential %	53.5	59.2	54.5	57.8
Ending presidential %	52.3	50.2	56.2	54.6

To begin with the limitations of the indicator, Table A.1 groups the results shown in Figure A.3 by whether the net career change (career Δ) was positive or negative and whether the open-seat to open-seat change (open Δ) was positive or negative. The results are also divided into the years 1900–1958 and 1960–2006. This division is different from previous ones used, but since the retirement slump began to increase in the 1960s, the grouping is done to isolate those years of a higher level from those with no increase.

This grouping makes the limitations of the indicator clear, and it also makes it clear what conditions create larger retirement slump scores. The middle two categories (career Δ −/open Δ − and career Δ +/open Δ +) indicate the limitations of the indicator. From 1900 to 1958, there were 342 cases in which the net career change was negative and the open-seat change was also negative. On average, members in this category lost 10.2 percentage points over their careers. Yet the partisan House vote dropped an average of 14.1 points compared to the prior open-seat contest, creating a positive retirement slump. The average presidential vote also declined from the initial open seat to open seat, dropping from 63.2 to 55.9. These members began with an average House vote percentage of 69.1 and ended with a House vote percentage of 58.8, and the partisan vote percentage in the next election was 54.9, resulting in a retirement slump of 3.9. Members and House districts in this category were experiencing both a personal and a general loss in partisan support for their party, but the general decline was greater than their personal decline, resulting in a positive retirement slump score. Members were losing support, but the calculation of the indicator suggests they had built up some advantage.

The next category (career Δ +/open Δ +) produces an equally odd result. These members gained support during their careers (13.3 points on average), but because the district was moving toward their party, the next open-seat percentage is higher, so the retirement slump, the difference between the last incumbent percentage and the next percentage, is 1.0. The average presidential vote also increased from the initial open seat to open seat. An incumbent who did well does not appear to have done so well because the general increase in partisan support was greater than the incumbent's personal gain.

These two categories (career Δ −/open Δ − and career Δ +/open Δ +) contain 68.1 percent of all cases from 1900 to 1958. They represent districts in which partisan change was occurring, and that partisan change was significantly altering the validity of the resulting retirement slump scores. If there had not been electoral change, the indicator might have been more reliable, but change diminished the connection between the experiences of incumbents and the retirement slump indicator.

The next category (career Δ −/open Δ +) might be regarded as that representing those politicians with limited skills. Of members, 8.8 percent had a negative career change, while the open-seat change was positive. These members began with a percentage of 64.4 and dropped to a percentage of 58.9, and the next open-seat percentage was 71.1. While the district was becoming more supportive of their party, these members were losing electoral support. Because the open-seat change was positive, it makes the retirement slump more negative, and the incumbents end up having a retirement slump that is considerably worse than what really occurred.

These three categories again indicate how questionable the retirement slump is as some sort of indicator of how an incumbent is able
to change electoral outcomes. There are, to be sure, cases in which
the open-seat to open-seat change is very limited and the net career
change and subsequent retirement slump are positive and reflect the
presumed effect of an incumbent, but those cases are in a distinct
minority. The process of open-seat changes enormously complicates
the meaning of the retirement slump indicator.

The concern here, however, is why the retirement slump increased
beginning in the 1960s. The last category is the most interesting and
relevant for understanding this change. These are cases in which the
incumbent vote percentage increased an average of 8.7 points, and the
next open seat declined by 8.5 percentage points from the prior open
seat percentage, creating a retirement slump of 16.9. These cases,
23 percent of all retiring members in the 1900–1958 time period,
clearly play a major role in creating an overall positive retirement
slump. The retirement slump for these cases is considerably higher
than for any other group. While 475 cases, or 39.6 percent of all cases,
are in the category of positive career change and positive open-seat
change, the average retirement slump in that category is only 1.0.
Whatever positive retirement slump result there is comes largely from
the last category of positive career changes and negative open-seat
changes.

What, then, changed in the latter time period that created a greater
retirement slump? First, the magnitude of electoral changes in all
categories increased. Net career increases and decreases were greater,
as were open-seat to open-seat shifts. Realignment was occurring, and
electoral shifts were greater. In the career Δ −/open Δ − category,
the open-seat to open-seat changes were −17.5 percentage points in
the latter time period, while they were −14.1 in the former.

The most important shift, however, was the shift in how many cases
were in different categories in the latter period. In the first time
period, 23 percent of cases were in the career Δ +/open Δ − category, the one generating the largest retirement slump scores. In the
latter time period, 36 percent of all cases were in that category. The
major change was in the category of cases in which the base partisan
support (measured by open seats) was shifting away from the party
(a negative open-seat change) but the incumbent was increasing his

or her vote percentage. There were more cases in this category, and there were greater electoral changes, creating much larger retirement scores. In the first time period the average career change was 8.7, and in the latter period it increased to 12.2. The open-seat to open-seat change increased from −8.5 to −11.1. The combination of greater electoral changes and more cases in this last category resulted in a significant increase in the overall retirement slump.

CAREER SUCCESS AND DECLINING PARTY FORTUNES

This category of career Δ +/open Δ − and the increase in the percentage of incumbents in the category from 1900–1958 to 1960–2006, might well be embraced by those arguing for an increased incumbency effect. The incumbents in this case bucked the shifts in partisan sentiments and increased their vote percentages, and there are more in the latter period than in the earlier. While there may be many incumbents whose vote percentages are moving with the partisan shifts (those in the career Δ −/open Δ − and career Δ +/open Δ + categories), there are now more incumbents able to improve their electoral fortunes despite the shifts in sentiments occurring. This category may only constitute 36 percent of all cases, but it is larger in the latter period and might be seen as indicative of a greater ability of incumbents to affect their vote percentages. Just as with the other indicators, the question is whether the numbers represent what they appear to represent.

Assessing changes in the category of career Δ +/open Δ − is best done by party since the changes occurring within each party are very different. Table A.2 presents the same groupings as in Table A.1, but only for 1960–2006 and by party. The Democratic retirement slump in the category of interest for these years is very high, at 24.7 percentage points. The presumption might be that this reflects the ability of Democratic incumbents to significantly increase their vote percentages during their careers. The simple view might be that once they depart, there is a significant drop in the partisan vote, creating this very large retirement slump. That is, however, not quite what happened. The average Democratic incumbent who left office during this time increased his or her vote percentage during his or her career by 12.2 percentage points. After incumbents left, the average partisan

TABLE A.2. *Retiring House member changes by party, 1960–2006*

	Career Δ +/ Open Δ −	Career Δ −/ Open Δ −	Career Δ +/ Open Δ +	Career Δ −/ Open Δ +
Democrats				
No. of cases	195	163	195	33
% all cases	33.3	27.8	33.3	5.6
Beginning House %	60.7	74.8	56.3	70.7
Ending House %	73.3	62.1	73.9	58.3
Career change	12.6	−13.0	17.6	−12.4
Next open seat %	48.2	55.0	71.6	77.6
Open-seat change	−12.3	−19.6	15.3	6.9
Retirement slump	24.7	6.9	2.4	−19.3
Beginning presidential %	50.6	59.9	53.4	57.0
Ending presidential %	49.4	48.6	56.7	58.5
Republicans				
No. of cases	181	85	176	18
% all cases	39.3	18.5	38.3	3.9
Beginning House %	56.1	62.3	53.4	57.4
Ending House %	67.6	56.3	70.3	53.7
Career change	11.5	−6.2	16.9	−3.6
Next open seat %	46.2	49.1	63.0	67.2
Open-seat change	−9.9	−13.4	9.7	9.9
Retirement slump	21.4	7.3	7.3	−13.5
Beginning presidential %	55.5	57.9	55.7	59.9
Ending presidential %	55.3	53.0	55.6	50.0

vote dropped by 12.1 percentage points from the previous open-seat contest. On average, half of the retirement slump score is because of the open-seat to open-seat change.

Why did such a large shift occur? These districts were ones in which the average presidential vote, an indicator of partisan dispositions,[1] when incumbents began their careers was 49.2.[2] These House candidates began their careers with vote percentages of 60.8 percent, or percentages that were 11.6 points higher than the presidential average. When they left office, the partisan percentage returned to levels equivalent to those being received by their presidential candidates, or

[1] A number of studies have assessed the relationship of presidential results with other indicators of liberal-conservative variations and found a strong relationship (Schwarz and Fenmore, 1977; Leogrande and Jeydel, 1997; Erikson and Wright, 2001).

[2] The number of cases for presidential results is limited because many of these incumbents were elected in non-presidential election years.

49.4 percent. A primary reason why there was such a large retirement slump for incumbents in this category is that they were beginning at a level well above what the presidential candidate was receiving. They were able to raise their vote percentages during their careers, but once they left, the next candidate from their party received the percentage the presidential district was receiving. In the case of retiring Democrats, it appears that the reason the open-seat to open-seat change was so large is because the prior Democrats were beginning with somewhat inflated percentages. As incumbents retired, the partisan percentages came closer to the partisan preferences indicated by presidential results.

The retiring Republican incumbents are less easy to assess. Thirty-nine percent of all retiring Republican candidates were in the category of career Δ +/open Δ −. These incumbents began with vote percentages very similar to those of their presidential candidates and increased their percentages by 11.5 points. When they retired, the vote for their party candidate in the next open-seat race dropped 9.9 points, creating a retirement slump of 21.4 percentage points. Presidential results in open-seat races following the retirement of a Republican candidate did not decline. General partisan support did not decline, but the partisan House vote did decline. Why that occurred is not clear, but it is clear that more retiring incumbents were in this situation and that the decline in partisan support from open seat to open seat is a major factor in the large retirement slumps in this group.

Again, there is much to learn about how the realignment process has affected the electoral results of incumbents. The impact of this process on the retirement slump is particularly complicated. The simplest finding that is evident regarding the retirement slump is that net career changes, open-seat to open-seat changes, and presidential result changes move together. That moving together renders the retirement slump score for many incumbents as not reflective of what has occurred in the district. For other incumbents, those in the career Δ +/open Δ − shift, the indicator produces an exaggerated score that is equally misleading. The important matter is that overall, the results move together, providing further evidence that there is a realignment process playing out that has a significant impact on our ability to estimate an incumbency advantage

The Gelman-King Analysis

One of the more commonly cited approaches to measuring the incumbency effect and its increase is that developed by Gelman and King (1990). The empirical results that their technique generates suggest that the incumbency effect began to increase in the 1960s and has remained relatively high since then. Given that their results indicate an increase and this book argues that there was not an increase, an analysis of their approach and results is in order.

Their concern is that existing measures of the incumbency effect (the sophomore surge and the retirement slump) are biased estimates.[1] By their calculation, the sophomore surge underestimates the

---

[1] The critique of their approach that follows focuses on the applied effects of their technique given the relationships among variables. While that is the concern, a comment is in order on the presumed problem they present. Their argument is apparently that there is *an* incumbency effect, and the sophomore surge and retirement slump are biased estimates of that general effect; that is, they are not equal empirically to the general effect. At various points Gelman and King (1990: 1142, 1144) suggest that selection bias is involved. This is not clarified, but presumably, they mean that the selective focus on the set of cases of first-reelection (the sophomore surge) incumbents or incumbents leaving (the retirement slump) involves focusing on an unrepresentative set of cases. Their argument is that a general indicator is unbiased. It is not clear to me that this is really a problem. Each of these indicators reflects a different aspect or phase of incumbency, and it seems that the differences they find are not a problem, but rather expected differences. The sophomore surge represents the first reelection bid of an incumbent and should be expected to be less than the average difference that all incumbents (many of long tenure) might achieve. A retiring member who has been in a lengthy number of years should surely have an advantage greater than the average of all incumbents (some with only two, four, or six years of service). The average incumbency effect should be expected to be between these two extremes. These different indicators may not be biased, but simply reflections of different stages of the incumbency effect. They may be trying to resolve a problem that is not really a problem. Having said that, the critique here is

incumbency advantage by about 2 percentage points and the retirement slump overestimates the incumbency effect by about 2 percentage points (Gelman and King, 1990: 1147–49):

> Even the most basic descriptive information about incumbency advantage is flawed because every previous measure based on aggregate data . . . is plagued by selection bias, inconsistencies, and inefficiencies. We prove this result and also propose a new unbiased and statistically efficient measure that is very easy to calculate. (Gelman and King, 1990: 1142)

They define the incumbency advantage for an entire legislature as "the average of the incumbency advantages for all districts in a general election" (Gelman and King, 1990: 1143). To address their concerns of reducing bias and increasing statistical efficiency (Gelman and King, 1990: 1142, 1145–49, 1151), they present the following variable specifications and equation:

> Denote v_1 and v_2 as the Democratic proportions of the two-party vote in elections 1 and 2, respectively. . . . Let I_1 equal 1 if a Democratic incumbent runs for reelection, 0 if no incumbent runs, and -1 if a Republican incumbent is seeking reelection. In addition, P_2 is 1 if the Democrat wins election 1 [the prior election], and -1 if the Republican wins.
>
> For a pair of election years, we base our measure of the incumbency effect ψ on a linear regression of votes on incumbency status, controlling for previous votes and partisan swing (Gelman and King, 1990: 1150–51).
>
> (Author comment: In this case I_1 is presented as a generic incumbent variable, but for this specific equation it is presented as I_2 to indicate that it is the incumbents running in year 2. While the discussion before the presentation of the equation mentions P_2 as if the winner in the second year is of relevance, the logic of the analysis is that the winner in the prior year is of interest, so the reference should be, I presume, to the winner in the prior year, or P_1, as in the above equation.)

$$E(v_2) = B_0 + B_1 v_1 + B_2 P_1 + \psi I_2$$

This technique, while initially discussed as being concerned with measuring the difference between the presence or absence of an

about the effects of Gelman and King's empirical analysis and not these conceptual issues.

incumbent within a single district and as an effort of "causal estimation with missing data" (Gelman and King, 1990: 1143–44), is really an
analysis within "a familiar regression framework" (Gelman and King,
1990: 1150). The Democratic vote percentage at t is regressed on
the Democratic vote percentage at t − 1. The prior vote percentage
is apparently intended as a control for the baseline vote in districts.
The prior winner is included as a control for partisan swing in the
national vote away from or toward Democrats from one year to the
next.[2] This variable allows the intercepts for Democrats and Republicans to vary. After these controls have operated, the remaining residual
scores for the current vote are associated with the incumbent variable.
Democratic incumbents are coded as 1, and Republican incumbents
are coded as −1. Districts with a zero incumbent code in the current year represent the absence of an incumbent. Democratic incumbents should produce positive residuals (an actual Democratic percentage greater than expected), and Republican incumbents should
have negative residuals (holding down the Democratic percentage

[2] While this is a very plausible variable to add, and I follow Gelman and King's (1990)
practice in the analyses that follow, there is also something odd about it. Their
argument is that there is a need to incorporate the national partisan swing. They
recognize that a member of Congress might be running in a year in which there is an
average partisan swing of 7 percentage points against her party across the country,
and this variable controls for this. The result is that we receive an estimation of
how an incumbent did, relative to the national swing. This can produce some odd
estimations of an incumbency effect. A Democratic member might experience a
decline of 6 percentage points but be presented as doing better, which is, in some
sense, correct, but it is odd to result in a positive score when the incumbent lost
votes. There is something very odd about saying that an incumbent is protected
from partisan swings with a personal electoral connection only if we calculate an
incumbency effect after controlling for a national swing. It is also possible that a
member could lose but be seen as having a positive incumbent score. Assume a
Democratic member receives 52 percent in 1964, and then there is a 7 percentage
point swing against Democrats. An incumbent Democrat could receive a positive
residual because he received 48 percent (having declined only 4 percentage points
rather than 7), and lost. It seems odd to use an estimation process that could report
a positive incumbency effect for a losing member.
   It is worth noting that this controlling for national swings conceals the extent to
which incumbents are affected by broad partisan swings in partisan support. It would
seem that if incumbents are successful in creating a personal connection with voters
that buffers them from broad partisan swings, they would then be less susceptible
to such swings, and their vote percentages would fluctuate less from year to year.
With that in mind, the following figure indicates the average partisan change for
Democratic and Republican incumbents from one election to the next. With few
exceptions, incumbents of both parties appear to experience the same fluctuations

greater than expected), so the coding results in 1 ∗ (positive residual) and −1 ∗ (negative residual). The result is that the residual results for the incumbent variable for both Democrats and Republicans end up being positive. Since both end up positive, they are folded together, and the incumbent coefficient ends up representing the average residual for all incumbents (Democrats and Republicans together) from the predicted current vote, controlling for prior percentage and winner.[3]

They estimate this equation for pairs of contested elections for successive two-year cycles. The results of this analysis are shown in Figure B.1.[4] As with their analysis, estimates are made only for changes

over time. It is difficult to see much evidence that the ability of incumbents to buffer themselves from partisan shifts has increased over time.

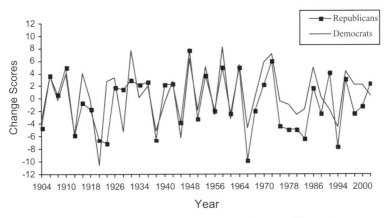

Year to year changes in Democratic vote percentages, by party of incumbent, 1904–2004.

---

[3] As Gelman and King (1990: 1143) note, they assume "that the incumbency advantage accruing to Democratic and Republican legislators is the same." This focus on the average effect of Democrats and Republicans has advantages and disadvantages. It focuses on the average incumbent without regard to party, simplifying the analysis to just incumbents. The disadvantage is that this neglects whether one party is doing better over time than another. It assumes no difference by party and thus forecloses assessing whether the effect was largely confined to one party, and is not a general effect for incumbents.

[4] For the years 1900–1990 I use the data set presented on King's Web site. For subsequent years I use data I compiled. There are three problems in replicating Gelman and King's (1990) results. First, they do not report their actual results, so it is difficult to know if I am faithfully replicating them. There is no table of the number of cases involved for each year, so I can only follow their logic and assume that I have generated results that are similar. It is also unclear about how some cases were

Figure B.1. Estimates of the incumbency effect, 1904–2000, using the Gelman-King method.

in years ending in 4, 6, 8, and o. Estimates are not generated for the pairs of years ending in o or 2 because reapportionment creates new districts in years ending in 2, and it is not possible to compare results for o and 2. Members are not running in the same districts,

handled. While they note that they are excluding uncontested cases, they do not specify whether the definition of *uncontested* is both the prior and current election or just the current. I chose the former definition, so a pair of elections (prior and current year) in which either major party candidate received no votes in either election is excluded. It is also unclear how at-large races are treated. For the incumbent variable they code at-large races as −9 (the traditional missing score code in many data sets), which I take to mean that they are excluded. While I see no reason to exclude at-large races since the size or nature of the district is not at issue, I follow what I take to be their pattern and exclude such races. Second, I should note that there are errors in the data set. There are numerous cases of a reported incumbent of a party when that is in error. I focus on 1966 because it is the first year in which a significant incumbency effect emerges. That year provides some examples of errors. They report (Gelman and King, 1990: 1157, n. 9) that they were able to "code incumbency by comparing the names of the winning candidates in successive elections." For whatever reasons, there are errors in the coding, and those errors are important. In Florida 8, Matthews (D) runs and wins in 1964, but he does not run in 1966. In their data set the district is coded as having an incumbent Republican candidate, when it should be an open seat. In New Jersey 12, Krebs (D) runs and wins in 1964, but he does not run in 1966. In their data set the district is coded as having an incumbent Republican candidate, when it should be an open seat. Third, it is not clear how some unique situations were handled. In 1964, in Florida 12, Cramer (R) won. In 1966 he ran in district 8, and Fascell (D) ran as an incumbent. It is not clear if Gelman and King merged 1964 and 1966 districts by state and district or by last name (implied in Gelman and King, 1990: 1157, n. 9). If the former was done, the coding for the prior winner would be in error. If the latter was done, this error might be corrected, assuming the coding so comparing results across those years is inappropriate. Beginning in 1966, there is a sustained and significant increase in the incumbency effect. The interpretation of these coefficients is important. The results indicate that, relative to the average partisan vote in a district, incumbents diverge from open-seat results by an average of 10–11 points in 1966. Over the next several decades, the average incumbency effect is roughly 8–9 percentage points.

THE DISJUNCTURE BETWEEN THEORY AND APPLICATION

The Gelman-King approach seems appropriate theoretically, and the regression analysis and results would *appear* to be plausible. They are proposing a relatively simple and typical regression analysis, in which a nominal variable picks up residuals of the current vote after controlling for various indicators. The results also seem plausible since other studies also show a growing incumbency effect beginning in the 1960s. If we use the internal logic of their proposed technique and the similarity of their results to other results as guides, it would seem there is little to doubt about the validity of their analysis and results.

Despite that presumption, the application of the technique generates results very different from what is presumed. While the technique is presented as if it tracks the ability of incumbents to boost their vote percentages, the actual results for the incumbency variable end up tracking changes in partisan vote percentages in open-seat races. The reason for this discrepancy between theory and application is technical in nature and will be explained next. The consequence is that the technique does not measure what it purports to measure and provides no supporting evidence for the conclusion offered.

The source of this discrepancy stems from the high multicollinearity that exists among the independent variables. The high correlation among the variables creates significant and unexpected problems. A relatively high Democratic vote in a House district in a prior election is typically followed by a relatively high Democratic vote in the next election. A prior Democratic winner in one election is highly likely

for 1964 was correctly incorporated. I merged districts by state and district number, which produces some obvious errors. There are only a few such errors, but, as will be discussed in the main text, they have some very significant consequences.

to be followed by a Democratic winner in the next election. Overall, districts are not erratic in their inclination to be Democratic or Republican from one election to another. The *relative* partisan position of districts generally does not change from one election to the next. The partisan vote may move $+5$ or -5 for all districts, but those heavily Republican tend to stay that way. This stability of relative partisanship means results from a prior election have a high association with results from a current election. It also leads to the partisan *winner* from a prior election having a high association with the partisan vote in the prior and current election. The result is that the correlation among the variables is so great that controlling for past partisan percentages *and* which party won leaves little residual variation in the current vote percentage.

The controlling process also leaves little variation in incumbent scores. For the incumbent variable the only unexpected variation occurs when a seat is open. It is only in these cases that there is any residual variation of any consequence. The result is an analysis in which the so-called incumbent coefficient is really assessing partisan change in open seats. While appearing to conduct an analysis of continuing incumbents, the Gelman-King analysis really tracks partisan changes in districts where incumbents are not present. Open seats are no longer some sort of zero point around which incumbent forces play out, but rather, they are the focus of the statistical analysis. *The important matter then becomes not what happens with partisan percentages for incumbents from year to year, but what happens from year to year in partisan percentages in open seats. Tracking changes in open seats from year to year becomes crucial to understanding what the Gelman-King analysis is following.*

Supporting these statements and explaining precisely what the Gelman-King approach does requires reviewing exactly what multiple regression does. Then a hypothetical example will be presented that indicates what happens when open-seat percentages change. The example indicates the importance of open-seat changes in calculating the incumbency advantage. Then a specific case of the Gelman-King analysis, using changes from 1964 to 1966, the first year in which the incumbency effect is large, is assessed. Going through what happens in the application of their approach is technical, but it is essential for understanding whether Gelman and King's (1990) results establish that the incumbency effect has grown. The problem with their approach is not the logic or the issue of bias, but what happens in the application of the technique. After the hypothetical case and the 1964–1966 changes are presented, an analysis of changes in incumbent and open-seat races over 100 years will be presented to further document the argument.

REGRESSION AND CONTROLS

The Gelman-King technique uses multiple regression, a technique that seeks to determine the independent effect of a condition (incumbency), controlling for the effect of other conditions. Republican incumbents are coded as -1 and Democratic incumbents are coded as 1. Open seats, when an incumbent chooses not to run, are coded as 0. To control an equation with three independent variables, this means, in effect, that first Y (Democratic percentage in year 2) is regressed on X_1 (Democratic percentage in year 1) and X_2 (winner in year 1). We are left with variation in Y independent of X_1 and X_2. Then X_3 (incumbency) is also regressed on X_1 and X_2. This gives us the variation in X_3 independent of X_1 and X_2. These remaining scores, or residuals, are then regressed on each other to derive the coefficient of b_{yx3}, or the independent effect of incumbent status on vote percentages.

If all the variables are highly correlated, this controlling process leaves little residual variation in year 2 scores (*if* stability of election results prevails from year to year, an issue to be taken up shortly). The exception and important matter regarding remaining residual variation after controls involves open seats. In cases in which incumbents run, the expected matches the actual (a Democrat (1) occurs in both years), and there are very small residual scores for the incumbency variable score. When an incumbent leaves and creates an open seat, it creates a significant discrepancy in the residual for the incumbent variable. An incumbent is expected (a 1 or -1), and the presence of an open seat (or 0) creates a significant residual, or difference between the expected and actual. By definition, the absence of an incumbent is a significant deviation from the expected.

If open seats constitute a significant residual for the incumbency score, then the other important matter is what happens in open seats

TABLE B.1. *Hypothetical data of changes from year 1 to year 2: incumbent scores and Democratic percentages of the vote*

| | | | | Democratic percentages | | | | | | |
| | Prior | Incumbent | Year 1 | Year 2 variations: unchanging incumbent scores with varying changes in open-seat percentages | | | | | | |
District	Winner	Code		1	2	3	4	5	6
1	1	0	61	61	59	57	55	53	51
2	1	1	59	63	63	63	63	63	63
3	1	1	57	59	59	59	59	59	59
4	1	1	55	58	58	58	58	58	58
5	−1	−1	45	42	42	42	42	42	42
6	−1	−1	43	41	41	41	41	41	41
7	−1	−1	41	37	37	37	37	37	37
8	−1	0	39	39	41	43	45	47	49
Average Democratic %			50.0	50.0	50.0	50.0	50.0	50.0	50.0
Average incumbent average			50.0	50.0	50.0	50.0	50.0	50.0	50.0

with partisan percentage changes from year to year. If they are stable (little change after an incumbent leaves), they provide, after controlling, no significant variation to associate with the residual incumbent scores. If they are not stable, and the extent of instability or change increases over time, then they create some residual variation to associate with open-seat scores. This issue is the heart of making sense of the Gelman-King technique.

A SIMULATED EXAMPLE

The consequence of all these matters – high correlations among the variables and the effects of open-seat changes – can be seen in the hypothetical example in Table B.1. The data set presents an example in which all incumbents running increase their vote percentages over their prior percentages. Democrats, coded as 1, increase their percentages an average of 3 points. Republicans, coded as −1, decrease the Democratic percentages an average of 3 points, improving the Republican average. The percentages that incumbents receive in every second year variation are the same. The only results that change are for open seats. For every simulated year 2 variation, the open-seat

TABLE B.2. *Regression results for data in table B.1*

Variables	Regression results by year 2 variations					
	1	2	3	4	5	6
With only 2 variables						
Prior %	1.0	.8	.7	.5	.3	.2
Incumbent	2.9	4.1	5.3	6.5	7.7	8.9
With 3 variables						
Prior %	1.3	1.3	1.3	1.3	1.3	1.3
Prior winner	−5.5	−9.5	−13.5	−17.5	−21.5	−25.5
Incumbent	4.0	6.0	8.0	10.0	12.0	14.0

percentage moves away by a greater amount from the partisan vote that prevailed when an incumbent ran.

Several matters are important to note about these data. First, in each year 2 variation, each incumbent does better than in year 1. Democratic incumbents improve their percentages, and Republican incumbents lower the percentages that Democratic challengers receive. Those improvements are constant across the example years. Each variation is set up to represent the possibility that incumbents improve their percentage by a uniform amount. Second, there is no shift in the national Democratic percentage from year to year. It was 50 percent in year 1 and remains at 50 percent in every year 2 example. Third, the only real change across the year variations is in the Democratic percentages in the open seats. In variation 1 in year 2, in the open seat, the Democratic percentage does not change from that received by the incumbent in the prior year. In each successive year 2 variation the open-seat percentage moves 2 more percentage points away from that received by the incumbent in year 1; that is, the partisan vote shifts away from the party that held the seat. Why that occurs is not of concern here. The concern is what happens in the Gelman-King analysis if that occurs. Fourth, the variables involved in the analysis all have high correlations with each other, with none being below .78.

Table B.2 indicates the effects of greater open-seat shifts on the incumbency variable and the effects of adding an additional variable. There are two sets of regression results. The first two rows (across, for

variation in year 2 conditions) present the regression coefficients for
a model using only the prior vote percentage and the incumbency
variables as independent variables. These results reflect the variation
in the incumbency variable as open-seat changes increase. The second
analysis (lower rows) add the variable of prior winner to assess the
impact of an additional variable.

The first set of results focuses on how the incumbency variable
changes as the open-seat percentages shift away from the prior year by
greater amounts. The initial year 2 variation (1) consists of an increase
in the vote percentage of each incumbent and no change in open-seat
results. If the analysis includes only the variables of the prior percentage and the incumbency variable, the results fit the conventional
expectation. The year 2 percentage has essentially a 1 to 1 relationship
with the prior percentage, and the incumbency variable picks up an
increase of almost 3 percentage points. The important matter is what
happens when the percentage in the open seat begins to shift relative to the vote received by the prior incumbent. Every greater shift
in the open-seat percentage, even with no change in incumbent percentages, results in an increase in the incumbency variable coefficient.
The greater the shift in the open seats, with no change in incumbent
performances, the greater the apparent so-called incumbency advantage. Nothing changed for incumbents, but the results look like their
fortunes improved.

Equally interesting is what happens when an additional variable
is added. The prior winner variable is included to pick up national
shifts in the vote. In this case, there is, by design, no change in the
national vote. Despite that, the coefficient for prior winner becomes
steadily larger as the open-seat shift increases. Most important is what
happens to the incumbency variable, with another highly correlated
independent variable included, as the open-seat changes occur. The
incumbency variable increases as the year 2 variations occur, and it
is bigger when another (highly correlated) variable is included. The
incumbency advantage is greater the larger the open-seat shift and the
more correlated variables are included in the analysis.

The source of the greater incumbency effect is not a change in
the situation of incumbents, but the effects of highly correlated variables. With highly correlated independent variables included, the only

residual variation in current vote percentages of any consequence left to examine involves open seats, and this creates the impression of a greater incumbency effect. This, of course, is a contrived example. The important matter is whether the pattern shown in Table B.2 has any relevance for what has occurred in House elections in recent decades.

ASSESSING ACTUAL CHANGES: 1964–1966

The year 1966 represents a year in which there was a major increase in the incumbency effect. Does this hypothetical example have relevance for what transpired in that year? This section assesses in detail the empirical relationships in 1964–1966. First, are the variables in these years highly correlated? The ability to predict X_3 (incumbency) from X_1 and X_2 is high. The R^2 of X_3 on the two variables is .86. If a district voted relatively strongly for a Democrat and a Democrat won, we would expect, given the relatively few retirements in any given year, that the candidate will be a Democratic incumbent. Likewise, if a Republican won and there was a strong vote for a Republican, we would expect to have a Republican incumbent present.

There were 25 districts in which an incumbent did not run. These cases are ones in which the deviation from the expected is significant. Table B.3 indicates just how much of a deviation occurs. It presents the results of the controlling process and the resulting residuals for the incumbency variable and for the open-seat percentages. Only contested seats are included, resulting in 360 districts. Not all cases are reported in the table, but all open seats and some illustrative incumbents are shown.

The actual variable data for the selected districts in 1964 and 1966 are shown in the first several columns. If the winner in 1964 was a Democrat, this is coded as 1, and if it was a Republican, this is coded as −1. The Democratic percentages in the district in 1964 and 1966 are next, followed by the actual change from 1964 to 1966. Perhaps the most important matter involves the residuals created when an incumbent runs or does not run. Again, when we control for prior Democratic percentage and who won in 1964, we regress the incumbency variable on these two variables. The result is the residual score for the incumbency variable independent of the 1964 conditions.

TABLE B.3. *Actual and predicted incumbency and 1966 Democratic vote scores, and residuals*

State	Dist.	Winner 1964	D% 1964	D% 1966	Δ 1964–1966	Incumbency scores			Democratic % 66	
						Coded	Predicted	Residual	Predicted	Residual
Open seats previously held by Democrats										
Wyoming	1	1	50.8	47.7	−3.1	0	1.0	−1.0	52.1	−4.4
N. Carolina	5	1	51.6	53.1	1.5	0	1.0	−1.0	52.4	0.6
Ohio	24	1	52.2	41.5	−10.7	0	1.0	−1.0	52.7	−11.2
Kentucky	3	1	53.8	41.0	−12.8	0	.9	−.9	53.4	−12.4
Georgia	5	1	54.0	39.9	−14.2	0	.9	−.9	53.5	−13.6
Texas	18	1	55.0	40.5	−14.4	0	.9	−.9	53.8	−13.3
Louisiana	6	1	62.9	76.6	13.7	0	.9	−.9	57.1	19.4
Pennsylvania	4	1	64.1	51.9	−12.2	0	.9	−.9	57.6	−5.7
Oregon	4	1	64.8	37.3	−27.5	0	.9	−.9	57.9	−20.6
Ohio	15	1	66.1	40.1	−26.0	0	.9	−.9	58.4	−18.4
New York	29	1	69.2	45.9	−4.5	0	.9	−.9	59.7	−13.9
Massachusetts	8	1	69.4	45.6	−23.8	0	.9	−.9	59.8	−14.2
New York	11	1	80.9	76.4	−4.5	0	.9	−.9	64.5	11.8
Texas	7	1	83.6	42.6	−41.0	0	.8	−.8	65.7	−23.0

Continuing incumbents: Republican and Democrat

Ohio	5	−1	34.1	24.7	−9.4	−1	−.9	−.1	31.1	−6.4
California	28	−1	34.4	27.7	−6.7	−1	−.9	−.1	31.2	−3.5
Washington	4	−1	34.7	32.8	−1.9	−1	−.9	−.1	31.3	1.5
Massachusetts	6	−1	35.4	34.3	−1.1	−1	−.9	−.1	31.6	2.7
New Jersey	3	1	50.4	53.0	2.6	1	−.9	0.0	52.0	1.1
New York	3	1	50.7	50.3	−0.4	1	1.0	0.0	52.1	−1.8
Pennsylvania	24	1	50.8	55.3	4.5	1	1.0	0.0	52.1	3.2
Wisconsin	6	1	50.8	47.6	−3.2	1	1.0	0.0	52.1	−4.5

Open seats previously held by Republicans

Indiana	7	−1	45.8	45.7	−.2	0	−.9	.9	35.9	9.8
Pennsylvania	7	−1	48.9	36.8	−12.1	0	−.9	.9	37.2	−0.4
Pennsylvania	8	−1	48.9	40.5	−8.5	0	−.9	.9	37.2	3.3
Pennsylvania	16	−1	35.9	30.8	−5.1	0	−.9	.9	31.8	−1.0
Alabama	7	−1	40.4	64.4	23.9	0	−.9	.9	33.7	30.7
Georgia	3	−1	42.6	61.8	19.2	0	−.9	.9	34.6	27.2
New Jersey	1	−1	43.7	47.4	3.7	0	−.9	.9	35.0	12.3
Mississippi	4	−1	44.3	66.7	22.4	0	−.9	.9	35.3	31.4
Maine	1	−1	48.9	52.7	2.7	0	−.9	.9	37.6	15.1
Massachusetts	10	−1	37.0	48.9	11.9	0	−.9	.9	32.3	16.6
Kansas	3	−1	37.8	46.0	8.1	0	−.9	.9	32.6	13.3

Winner 64 is coded as −1 for Republican and 1 for Democrat; D% 64 and D% 66 are actual percentage of the two-party vote; Δ 1964–1966 is 1964–1966; incumbent 66 is the coding for whether a Republican (−1) or Democratic (1) incumbent was present; predicted scores are from regressing D% 66 and incumbent 66 on D% 64 and winner 64. All data are from King's Web site (http://gking.harvard.edu/projects/inc.shtml).

When an incumbent runs, the difference of the actual code from the predicted score is very small. These cases are shown in the middle of the table.

The three columns under "Incumbency scores" show initial codes and then predicted and residual results. The coded incumbency status scores are 1 for D incumbent, −1 for R incumbent, and 0 for open seat. The predicted scores are based on regressing incumbency scores on the 1964 winner and the 1964 Democratic percentage. The difference between the actual and predicted is the residual in the third column. When an open seat occurs, the residuals for the incumbency variable are, relatively speaking, very large. This is because when a Democrat won in 1964, we would expect a Democratic incumbent to be present (a score of 1), and an actual score of 0 (no incumbent at all present) is a significant divergence from what is expected. When a Republican won in 1964 but the seat is open in 1966, there is also a significant residual. In Wyoming 1, the regression predicts that the incumbent in 1966 should be a Democrat (1), but with none present (0), the actual is 1 below the expected, so the actual score is a deviation −1 below what we expected, or in simple language, there is a relatively high error. We expected a Democratic incumbent but there is not one, so the prediction is way off. In Kansas 3 (bottom of table), we expect a Republican incumbent (−.9) and get none, or a 0, so the actual is .9 higher than expected, or a relatively large residual.

The result of this controlling process is that all cases in which an incumbent is expected and does exist have near-zero residuals for the incumbency variable after controlling. Significant variation from zero occurs only when an open seat exists. Cases where a Democrat incumbent should be present create negative residuals, and cases where a Republican incumbent should be present create positive residuals.

While the Gelman-King approach creates large residuals for open seats, what happens with partisan vote percentages in those cases? The other half of the analysis involves what happens with vote percentages after we control for prior political conditions (X_1 and X_2). To derive these residuals, or scores independent of the effects of X_1 and X_2, we also need to have 1966 Democratic residual scores after controlling for the 1964 winner and Democratic percentage. The actual 1966 results and the residuals are shown in the last two columns of Table B.3. The

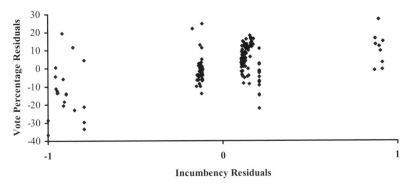

Figure B.2. Residuals for Democratic vote percentage and incumbency, pairing the 1964 and 1966 elections.

effect of not having an incumbent present is again important. When a Democratic incumbent vacates (the top rows), the 1966 Democratic percentage diverges from the predicted (based on 1964 results). The actual percentage is considerably less than expected, and the residuals are relatively large negatives. When a Republican incumbent vacates in 1966 (the bottom rows), the actual Democratic percentage diverges from the predicted (based on 1964 results) and is considerably greater than expected, and the residuals are relatively large positive scores. When an incumbent chooses to run, the actual is much closer to the expected, and the deviations or residuals are relatively small. For both incumbent and Democratic percentages, the crucial factor affecting the size of the residuals is whether an open seat occurs.

This review gets us to the covariation of the residuals for the incumbency and vote percentages variables. This covariation has served as the basis for this approach to analyzing the incumbency effect. The resulting pattern of covariation among residual scores for 1966 is shown in the scatterplot of Figure B.2. When an incumbent runs (either Democrat or Republican), the predicted incumbent score is essentially the same as the actual score, so the residuals are very small deviations from 0, ranging from −.2 to .2. These residuals (along the horizontal axis) cluster in the middle of the scatterplot. The crucial residuals are those involving cases of open seats. When a Republican retires, the result is a positive residual for the incumbency score of .8 or .9, which is to the far right in the scatterplot. When a Democrat retires, the result is a negative residual of −.8 to −1, which is to the far

TABLE B.4. *Average Democratic percentage residuals grouped by incumbency category, 1964–1966*

Incumbency category	Range of residual scores	N	Average Democratic % residual
Retiring Democrat	<−.7	21	−14.6
Continuing Democrat	−.3–<0	122	−1.7
Continuing Republican	0–.2	219	1.4
Retiring Republican	>.7	13	15.9

left in the scatterplot. As noted previously, the residuals for the cases in which a Democratic incumbent vacated are negative, and when a Republican vacated, they are positive.

For the 1966 analysis, there are 25 open seats. They have large residuals on the incumbency variable and are the cases to the left and right.[5] Whatever relationship exists between the incumbent and 1966 Democratic percentage residuals comes from the variation surrounding the open-seat cases and not from what is happening with continuing incumbents. The continuing incumbent scores all cluster in the middle, and these cases have no impact on creating an apparent incumbency effect.

Table B.4 summarizes the results in Figure B.2. The table presents residuals for the 1966 Democratic vote percentage grouped by the

---

[5] In addition, there are five cases that are errors, using the data King posted on his Web site. For the 1964–1966 data, five districts have incorrect scores recorded, which leads to errors. In addition to the large residuals created by open seats, there are also large residuals created by the presence of special elections. If a Republican wins a race in 1964 (prior winner = −1), then leaves office and is replaced by a Democrat in 1965 in a special election, the incumbent coding for 1966 will be 1. The estimated incumbent score will be close to −1, so there will be a significant positive residual. If a Democrat wins in 1964 (prior winner = 1) but changes parties in 1965, and is coded as an incumbent Republican, there will be another large residual. Finally, if an incumbent experiences reapportionment between 1964 and 1966 and occupies a district with a different number by 1966, the merger of results by district number may create the same problems. It only takes a few such changes to create a scatterplot and a relationship like that in Figure B.2. Almost every two-year cycle creates such changes. From 1904 through 2004, there are only a few years in which no such changes occur. The actual number of such situations ranges from 1 to 15. Retaining such situations in the analysis produces estimations of the incumbency effect that are really estimations driven by these kinds of changes in partisan situations. Dealing with them is not simple. They cannot simply be recoded because if a Democrat won in 1964 and a Republican incumbent exists (via a special election), that is an accurate coding of the situation.

status of the candidates in the race. For each incumbent status the range of residuals is presented in the first column. The last column presents the average residual for the Democratic vote percentage for 1966. For retiring Democrats (residuals on the left in Figure B.2) the average residual is −14.6. Vote percentages were considerably below what was expected. For retiring Republicans (residuals on the right in Figure B.2) the average residual is 15.9, or much higher than expected. While the residuals for continuing incumbents cluster in the middle, those for retiring incumbents diverge from the others, and their relative values create a so-called relationship between incumbency residuals and Democratic percentage residuals. The effect of controlling is that we end up with a so-called change in average Democratic residuals from −14.6 to 15.9 as the incumbency residual varies from −1 to .9. The result for that year is a very large regression coefficient for incumbent status. While that has been interpreted as reflecting a large incumbency effect, it is really an indicator that large shifts in open seats occurred that year.

As odd as it may seem, an analysis that begins with a focus on the incumbency effect ends up focusing on variation in vote percentages in open seats. In the 1964–1966 analysis, we derive a coefficient of approximately 10 for b_{yx3}, controlling for other conditions. It appears that an incumbency effect of 10 percentage points exists. The reality is that this much noted incumbency effect is a reflection of changes in open seats and not of what is happening with incumbents. If the discussion were to focus on changes in open seats, as will be the case in the following section, there might be some basis for salvaging the results, but incumbents play a role in the Gelman-King analysis only by their absence.

THE OPEN-SEAT ISSUE

The 1964–1966 analysis involves changes from one pair of elections. It suggests that the Gelman-King analysis is really an assessment of what happened in open-seat races over 100 years. If that is the case, then we should see a pattern of changes in open-seat results that correspond in time with the rise in the incumbency effect that they report. It should be the case that changes in open-seat results from the prior

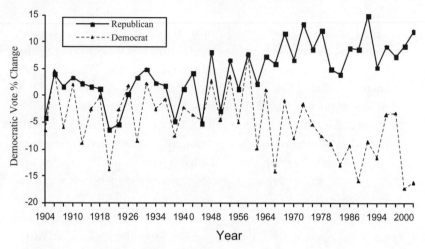

Figure B.3. Actual Democratic vote changes in open seats by prior party winner, 1904–2004.

partisan results begin to increase at the same time that the presumed incumbency effect begins to increase.

Figure B.3 presents the actual (not residual) average change in partisan vote percentages for open seats by the party of the prior winner from 1904 through 2004. Something clearly happened beginning in the 1960s. The partisan vote in open seats began to shift much more than in prior years. A positive score for a retiring Republican incumbent means that after a Republican incumbent retired the results became less Republican (more Democratic) in the next election. A negative score for a retiring Democratic incumbent means that after a Democratic incumbent retired the results became more Republican (less Democratic) when the incumbent left. Open-seat changes became greater beginning in the 1960s, and given their determining role in the Gelman-King analysis, it is this change that creates the statistical result that the incumbency effect has been increasing.[6]

Up until the 1960s, when an incumbent from either party retired, the partisan vote percentages for the retiring Republican and the

---

[6] This might prompt an argument that the retirement slump was increasing and, despite the problems with the analysis, it is still picking up a significant change in House elections. That largely changes the analysis from incumbents to nonincumbents. More important, there is a problem, as discussed in Chapter 5, with interpreting the retirement slump. Appendix A addresses this issue in greater detail.

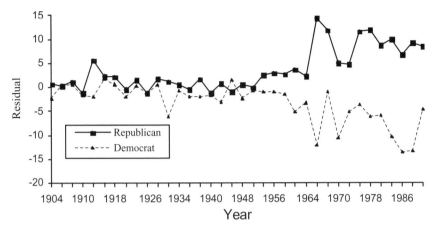

Figure B.4. Average residuals for Democratic vote percentages in open seats by prior party winner, 1904–1999.

next Republican did not differ much. If, for example, a Republican got 65 percent in her last election, the next Republican candidate, on average, did not differ much from that. Beginning in the 1960s, a significant change occurred. The level of partisanship that had prevailed was, on average, not sustained in the next level. After the 1960s, average Democratic percentages increased much more when Republican incumbents retired, and the average Democratic percentages decreased much more when a Democratic incumbent retired.

To assess the possibility that there was a change in the residuals for current (or year 2) vote percentages in cases of open seats beginning in the 1960s, the procedure just reviewed for 1964–1966 was repeated for all years from 1900 to 1990 using the data King posted on his Web site. For each year the vote percentage was regressed on the prior vote percentage and the prior winner. The residuals for continuing incumbents were then grouped by whether the incumbent was a Democrat or Republican and averaged within each group. There is little change over time in these average residuals.[7]

The residuals for open seats were then grouped by whether the exiting incumbent was a Republican or Democrat and averaged within each group. These are shown in Figure B.4. Republican residuals (deviations of the actual Democratic vote from the expected) are positive

[7] The results for this analysis are available from the author on request.

and the Democratic residuals (deviations) are negative. Beginning
in the 1960s, something happened to average scores. From 1904
through 1950, there were minor changes in partisan percentages
when an incumbent left the seat. From 1954 through 1964 the deviations increased. Then, in 1966, relatively large deviations from the
expected began to occur, and they have persisted. The deviations were
systematic, with votes in seats held by Republicans moving Democratic
and votes in seats held by Democrats moving Republican.

As noted in the analysis of the 1964–1966 case, the residuals for
the incumbency variable for Republicans are positive and those for
Democrats are negative. The result is that in a scatterplot of incumbency status residuals with partisan vote percentage residuals, the negative incumbency residuals (cases of Democrats retiring) will be associated with negative vote percentage residuals (the lower left corner),
and the positive incumbency residuals (cases of Republicans retiring)
will be associated with positive vote percentage residuals (the upper
right corner), which will create an apparent positive incumbency variable result. The result of the open-seat residuals becoming bigger
and separating, as just discussed, is that beginning in the 1950s, and
becoming much more pronounced in the 1960s, the regression slope
for the incumbency variable increases fairly dramatically, reflecting
the partisan changes in open seats.

There is a great deal of work that we need to do to understand why
these open-seat changes were occurring. It is very likely that this emergence of change in the 1950s–1960s reflects the secular realignment
that was beginning in earnest during those decades, but it is clear
that the major changes affecting the Gelman-King estimation of the
incumbency effect were what was happening in open-seat races and
not what was happening with incumbents.

The Data Set

The creation of a reasonably correct data set for both House and presidential election results was fairly involved. While I would like to state that the results are absolutely correct, I still occasionally find an error. Furthermore, as will be noted in the following sections, there can be disputes about what a so-called correct score is for some elections. First, the creation of the House data set will be discussed, and then the presidential data set will be discussed.

HOUSE ELECTION RESULTS

With regard to House results, I relied on Michael J. Dubin's (1998) *United States Congressional Elections, 1788–1997*. This work allowed the correction of several kinds of error that show up in Inter-University Consortium for Political and Social Research (ICPSR) data files.

One kind of so-called error is particularly noteworthy. In both California and New York, cross-endorsement of candidates has occurred, and continues to exist in New York. In California a candidate might run with the endorsement of the Democratic and Republican parties. In these cases Dubin (1998) records the votes cast on each party endorsement line of a candidate. I was able to verify the actual party affiliation (not endorsements) of candidates by checking their affiliations in the prior Congress, using either results for prior elections or by consulting the Biographical Directory of the United States Congress (http://bioguide.congress.gov/biosearch/biosearch.asp). In the ICPSR data set, many of these districts have no recorded votes, and these districts end up missing in analyses of vote percentages.

In New York, candidates can be cross-endorsed and then have their names listed on both lines. I checked these cases against the official results printed in the *Legislative Manual* for various years. While the votes on the separate lines should be added together and recorded as only a Democratic or Republican vote, the ICPSR data set records the vote on the Democratic line as the vote for a Democratic candidate and the vote on the Republican line as the vote for a Republican candidate. The result is that a district is recorded as contested and competitive to some degree, when in fact it was uncontested by a major party candidate. Races were recorded as closer than they were. In both of these states I corrected the data. In California I used Dubin's (1998) or the Biographical Directory designation of the candidate's actual party affiliation and recorded the total votes for the candidate on all party lines on the candidate's true party line. The other party line was given a zero. The logic of this is that the general concern is the partisan vote for major party candidates. In each district, almost all candidates will have an initial party affiliation, and that will be known in the district. If the candidate receives the endorsement of another party, the actual vote is still for a candidate of a specific party. In New York the same logic applies. While a name is listed on two (or more) lines, the party affiliation of each candidate is well known, and the vote is for that candidate, regardless of on which line it is received.

A similar issue involves Minnesota voting. For years the Democrat-Farmer-Labor (DFL) Party served as the vehicle for representing the Democratic Party in the state. The ICPSR shows no vote for Democratic candidates in the years that the DFL was relevant. We recorded the DFL percentages as the Democratic vote. Again, the concern is not the vote percentage recorded on a party line, but the vote percentage that a candidate of a major party received.

Results in Louisiana present a particularly difficult issue of how to record results. For some years Louisiana held an open primary, in which all party candidates could enter. If no candidate received a majority, a runoff would be held between the two candidates with the highest percentages, even if they were in the same party. If a candidate did receive a majority, the individual would appear on the ballot on the traditional Tuesday in November without any apparent opposition. There would then be no recorded votes, making it difficult to record a result. If a candidate received enough votes to avoid a runoff, the apparent result in November is 0 (no votes) or 100 percent, for no opponent. Neither option may reflect the vote proportion that the candidate won in the open primary. In a study of vote percentages of members of Congress, the options of 0 or 100 percent are not satisfactory indicators of the situation the candidate faced.

These races might simply be excluded, but that also is not very satisfactory. An option is to return to the results from Dubin (1998), which present both the open primary and runoff results. In many of these districts, several Democrats ran along with several Republicans, and the winning percentage might be, for example, only 30 percent, compared to 13 percent for a Republican. Since, in this particular study, the concern is the vote proportion of candidates and their relative security, the decision in this case is to record the percentages of the leading Democrat and the leading Republican. This is not completely satisfactory since the leading Democrat might receive 30 percent, followed by a Democrat with 22 percent, and then a Republican with 14 percent. Recording only the leading Democrat and Republican will underrepresent the closeness of the second highest vote recipient. That is, however, also a potential issue in a state like California, where the second highest vote recipient could run on the Progressive Party, and not show up if only Democrats or Republicans are recorded. While this is a problem, it is minor because the focus in these vote records is on the proportion of winners, and the practice of recording 30 percent and 14 percent will reflect the percentage of the winner. The virtue of recording these percentages is that the winner actually received only 30 percent, which is not a secure position. Accurately recording and reflecting that low percentage seems appropriate in this case, and this is what was done. If a candidate was unopposed in the open primary, the candidate is recorded as unopposed and as receiving 100 percent.

The problems in California and Minnesota may not affect results for members of Congress, if those researchers doing data runs took care to record the votes of winners, regardless of the party lines involved. If, on the other hand, a district were recorded as having a Democratic or Republican winner, but no percentages are recorded on the Democratic or Republican lines, then these districts may show up as missing in analyses. It is not possible to tell if this occurred because most studies contain no discussions of these specifics. In New York the problem could create clear errors of percentages. If a cross-endorsed Democrat in New York City has his or her vote across two lines, his or her vote proportion might be interpreted as 65 percent, when the actual percentage is 95 percent, and there is no major opponent. If only contested races are assessed, the New York situation will lead to this district being included, when it should have been excluded. Again, it is unknown whether this problem actually occurred in published studies because there is no discussion of such issues.

There is also an important issue about how to record at-large contests when there are multiple seats involved. While the winners can easily be recorded, there is the issue of what percentages to record for the winner and the opponent. The goal here is to record the competitiveness of elections, so with that in mind, the winner with the highest percentage is recorded and paired with the major party losing opponent with the highest percentage. The next highest winner is paired with the next highest major party losing candidate. For example, in Illinois in 1916, the winning Republican, McCormick, was given 54.4 percent and was paired with the most successful losing Democrat, Williams, with 42.0 percent.

There are a number of contested elections. If someone was listed as winning in the initial counts, but an investigation resulted in a corrected outcome and corrected score, the corrected results were recorded, rather than the initial results.

Dubin (1998) was also used as a basis for recording special elections and for exits before the end of a term. He reports special elections for each Congress. These results were entered to make sure that when a member entered via a special election, the beginning of a career was the special and not the next general election. Dubin's data were also used to indicate the end of a career, regardless of how it ended. Special election results for years after Dubin's records were obtained from the Clerk of the U.S. House of Representatives (http://clerk.house.gov/).

PRESIDENTIAL ELECTION RESULTS

The presidential election results were taken largely from two sources. Results from 1952 through 2000 were taken from various

Congressional Quarterly (CQ) reference books or reports or other sources such as the annual *Almanac of American Politics* for various years. In some years CQ reported the results in March of the year following the presidential election. In other cases CQ published the results in *Congressional Districts in the 1980s* (Washington, DC: Congressional Quarterly, 1983) or *Congressional Districts in the 1990s* (Washington, DC: Congressional Quarterly, 1993). For a few years the results were available only in editions of the *Almanac of American Politics*. The 2000 results were obtained directly from CQ. The results for 1900–1948 come from a project Peter Nardulli has been working on. He compiled data on presidential results by county, and using information from Kenneth C. Martis's (1982) *The Historical Atlas of United States Congressional Districts, 1789–1983* on which counties comprise each House district, it was possible to aggregate county presidential results to the congressional district level and have presidential results by congressional district. A complete explanation of how these data were compiled is available from him at the University of Illinois. I greatly appreciate his willingness to share these data.

Bibliography

Abramowitz, Alan I. 1975. "Name Familiarity, Reputation and the Incumbency Effect in a Congressional Election." *Western Political Quarterly*. Vol. 28, No. 4 (December): 668–84.

———. 1989. "Campaign Spending in U.S. Senate Elections." *Legislative Studies Quarterly*. Vol. 14, No. 4 (November): 487–507.

———. 1991. "Incumbency, Campaign Spending, and the Decline of Competition in U.S. House Elections." *Journal of Politics*. Vol. 53, No. 1 (February): 34–56.

Abramowitz, Alan I., and Kyle L. Saunders. 1998. "Ideological Realignments in the U.S. Electorate." *Journal of Politics*. Vol. 60, No. 3 (August): 634–52.

Aldrich, John H. 1995. *Why Parties: The Origin and Transformation of Party Politics in America*. Chicago: University of Chicago Press.

Alford, John R., and John R. Hibbing. 1981. "Increased Incumbency Advantage in the House." *Journal of Politics*. Vol. 43, No. 4 (November): 1042–61.

Andersen, Kristi. 1979. *The Creation of the Democratic Majority 1928–1936*. Chicago: University of Chicago Press.

Ansolabehere, Stephen, James M. Snyder Jr., and Charles Stewart III. 2000. "Old Voters, New Voters, and the Personal Vote: Using Redistricting to Measure the Incumbency Advantage." *American Journal of Political Science*. Vol. 44, No. 1 (January): 17–34.

Bartels, Larry M. 2000. "Partisanship and Voting Behavior, 1952–1996." *American Journal of Political Science*. Vol. 44, No. 1 (January): 35–49.

Bensel, Richard F. 2000. *The Political Economy of American Industrialism, 1877–1900*. New York: Cambridge University Press.

Black, Earl, and Merle Black. 1987. *Politics and Society in the South*. Cambridge, MA: Harvard University Press.

———. 1992. *The Vital South*. Cambridge, MA: Harvard University Press.

————. 2002. *The Rise of Southern Republicans.* Cambridge, MA: Harvard University Press.

Bond, Jon R. 2001. "A Silver Anniversary Retrospective on David Mayhew's *Congress: The Electoral Connection.*" *PS: Political Science and Politics.* Vol. 34, No. 2 (June): 253–54.

Born, Richard. 1979. "Generational Replacement and the Growth of Incumbent Reelection Margins in the U.S. House." *American Political Science Review.* Vol. 73, No. 3 (September): 811–17.

Brady, David W., John F. Cogan, and Morris P. Fiorina. 2000. "An Introduction." In David W. Brady, John F. Cogan, and Morris P. Fiorina, eds., *Continuity and Change in House Elections.* Stanford, CA: Stanford University Press: 1–9.

Brady, David W., Robert D'Onofrio, and Morris P. Fiorina. 2000. "The Nationalization of Electoral Forces Revisited." In David W. Brady, John F. Cogan, and Morris P. Fiorina, eds., *Continuity and Change in House Elections.* Stanford, CA: Stanford University Press: 130–48.

Breaux, David A. 1990. "Specifying the Impact of Incumbency on State Legislative Elections: A District-Level Analysis." *American Politics Quarterly.* Vol. 18, No. 3 (July): 270–86.

Brennan, Mary C. 1995. *Turning Right in the Sixties: The Conservative Capture of the GOP.* Chapel Hill: University of North Carolina Press.

Brewer, Mark D., and Jeffrey M. Stonecash. 2007. *Split: Class and Cultural Divides in American Politics.* Washington, DC: CQ Press.

————. 2009. *The Dynamics of American Political Parties.* New York: Cambridge University Press.

Burnham, Walter Dean. 1965. "The Changing Shape of the American Political Universe." *American Political Science Review.* Vol. 59, No. 1 (March): 7–28.

————. 1970. *Critical Elections and the Mainsprings of American Politics.* New York: W. W. Norton.

————. 1975. "Insulation and Responsiveness in Congressional Elections." *Political Science Quarterly.* Vol. 90, No. 3 (Fall): 411–35.

Campbell, James E. 1983. "The Return of the Incumbents: The Nature of the Incumbency Advantage." *Western Political Quarterly.* Vol. 36, No. 3 (September): 434–44.

Carson, Jamie L., Erik J. Engstrom, and Jason M. Roberts. 2007. "Candidate Quality, the Personal Vote, and the Incumbency Advantage in Congress." *American Political Science Review.* Vol. 101, No. 2 (May): 289–302.

Carter, Dan T. 1995. *The Politics of Rage: George Wallace, the Origins of the New Conservatism and the Transformation of American Politics.* Baton Rouge: Louisiana State University Press.

Collie, Melissa P. 1981. "Incumbency, Electoral Safety, and Turnover in the House of Representatives, 1972–1976." *American Political Science Review.* Vol. 75, No. 1 (March): 119–31.

Congressional Quarterly. 2001. *Congressional Quarterly's Guide to U.S. Elections,* 4th ed. Washington, DC: CQ Press.

Converse, Philip E. 1976. *The Dynamics of Party Support.* Beverly Hills, CA: Sage.

Cover, Albert. 1977. "One Good Term Deserves Another: The Advantage of Incumbency in Congressional Elections." *American Journal of Political Science.* Vol. 21, No. 3 (August): 523–41.

Cover, Albert D., and David R. Mayhew. 1977. "Congressional Dynamics and the Decline of Competitive Congressional Elections." In Lawrence C. Dodd and Bruce I. Oppenheimer, eds., *Congress Reconsidered.* Washington, DC: CQ Press: 62–82.

Cox, Gary, and Jonathan Katz. 1996. "Why Did the Incumbency Advantage Grow?" *American Journal of Political Science.* Vol. 40, No. 2 (May): 478–97.

Cox, Gary W., and Scott Morgenstern. 1993. "The Increasing Advantage of Incumbency in the U.S. States." *Legislative Studies Quarterly.* Vol. 18, No. 4 (November): 495–514.

Cummings, Milton C. 1966. *Congressmen and the Electorate.* New York: Free Press.

Degler, Carl N. 1964. "American Political Parties and the Rise of the City: An Interpretation." *Journal of American History.* Vol. 51, No. 1 (June): 41–59.

Dionne, E. J. 1997. *They Only Look Dead.* New York: Touchstone.

Dodd, Lawrence. 2001. "Comments on David Mayhew's *Congress: The Electoral Connection.*" *PS: Political Science and Politics.* Vol. 34, No. 2 (June): 262–64.

Dubin, Michael J. 1998. *United States Congressional Elections, 1788–1997.* Jefferson, NC: McFarland.

Edwards, Lee. 1999. *The Conservative Revolution.* New York: Free Press.

Edwards, George C., III, Martin P. Wattenberg, and Robert L. Lineberry. 2004. *Government in America,* 11th ed. New York: Pearson Longman.

Erikson, Robert S. 1971. "The Advantage of Incumbency in Congressional Elections." *Polity.* Vol. 3, No. 3 (Spring): 395–405.

———. 1972. "Malapportionment, Gerrymandering and Party Fortunes in Congressional Elections." *American Political Science Review.* Vol. 66, No. 4 (March): 1234–45.

———. 1976. "Is There Anything Such as a Safe Seat?" *Polity.* Vol. 8, No. 4 (Summer): 623–32.

Erikson, Robert S., and Gerald C. Wright. 2001. "Voters, Candidates, and Issues in Congressional Elections." In Lawrence C. Dodd and Bruce I.

Oppenheimer, eds., *Congress Reconsidered*, 7th ed. Washington, DC: CQ Press: 67–95.

Fenno, Richard F., Jr. 1978. *Home Style: House Members in Their Districts.* New York: HarperCollins.

Ferejohn, John A. 1977. "On the Decline of Competition in Congressional Elections." *American Political Science Review.* Vol. 71, No. 1 (March): 166–76.

Fiorina, Morris. 1973. "Electoral Margins, Constituency Influence, and Policy Moderation: A Critical Assessment." *American Politics Quarterly.* Vol. 1, No. 4 (October): 479–98.

———. 1977a. "The Case of the Vanishing Marginals: The Bureaucracy Did It." *American Political Science Review.* Vol. 71, No. 1 (March): 177–81.

———. 1977b. *Congress: Keystone to the Washington Establishment.* New Haven, CT: Yale University Press.

———. 1980. "The Decline of Collective Responsibility in American Politics." *Daedalus.* Vol. 9, No. 1 (Summer): 25–45.

———. 1981. "Some Problems in Studying the Effects of Resource Allocation in Congressional Elections." *American Journal of Political Science.* Vol. 25, No. 3 (August): 543–67.

Flanigan, William H., and Nancy H. Zingale. 1979. *Political Behavior of the American Electorate.* Boston: Allyn and Bacon.

Froman, Lewis A., Jr. 1963a. *Congressmen and Their Constituencies.* Chicago: McNally.

———. 1963b. "Inter-party Constituency Differences and Congressional Voting Behavior." *American Political Science Review.* Vol. 57, No. 1 (March): 57–61.

Garand, James C. 1991. "Electoral Marginality in State Legislative Elections, 1968–1986." *Legislative Studies Quarterly.* Vol. 16, No. 1 (February): 7–28.

Garand, James C., and Donald A. Gross. 1984. "Changes in the Vote Margins for Congressional Candidates: A Specification of Historical Trends." *American Political Science Review.* Vol. 78, No. 1 (March): 17–30.

Gardner, Michael. 2003. *Harry Truman and Civil Rights: Moral Courage and Political Risks.* Carbondale: Southern Illinois University Press.

Gelman, Andrew, and Zaiying Huang. Forthcoming. "Estimating Incumbency Advantage and Its Variation as an Example of a Before-After Study." *Journal of the American Statistical Association.* http://www.stat.columbia.edu/~gelman/research/published/inc6.pdf (accessed May 2007).

Gelman, Andrew, and Gary King. 1990. "Estimating Incumbency Effect without Bias." *American Journal of Political Science.* Vol. 34, No. 4 (November): 1142–64.

Ginsberg, Benjamin, Theodore J. Lowi, and Margaret Weir. 2005. *We the People: An Introduction to American Politics*, Shorter 5th ed. New York: W. W. Norton.

Green, John C., Lyman A. Kellstedt, Corwin E. Smidt, and James L. Guth. 1998. "The Soul of the South: Religion and the New Electoral Order." In Charles S. Bullock III and Mark J. Rozell, *The New Politics of the Old South*. Boulder, CO: Rowman and Littlefield: 261–276.

Griffin, John D. 2006. "Electoral Competition and Democratic Responsiveness: A Defense of the Marginality Hypothesis." *Journal of Politics*. Vol. 68, No. 4 (November): 911–21.

Gross, Donald A., and James C. Garand. 1984. "The Vanishing Marginals, 1824–1980." *Journal of Politics*. Vol. 46, No. 1 (February): 224–37.

Gujarati, Damodar N. 2003. *Basic Econometrics*, 4th ed. New York: McGraw-Hill.

Hibbing, John R. 1991. *Congressional Careers: Contours of Life in the U.S. House of Representatives*. Chapel Hill: University of North Carolina Press.

Herrnson, Paul S. 2004. *Congressional Elections: Campaigning at Home and in Washington*, 4th ed. Washington, DC: CQ Press.

Hodgson, Godfrey. 1996. *The World Turned Right Side Up*. Boston: Mariner Books.

Hofstadter, Richard. 1955. *The Age of Reform: From Bryan to F.D.R.* New York: Random House.

Hurley, Patricia A. 2001. "David Mayhew's *The Electoral Connection* after 25 Years." *PS: Political Science and Politics*. Vol. 34, No. 2 (June): 259–60.

Jacobson, Gary C. 1978. "The Effects of Campaign Spending in Congressional Elections." *American Political Science Review*. Vol. 72, No. 2 (June): 469–91.

———. 1983. *The Politics of Congressional Elections*. Boston: Little, Brown.

———. 1985. "Money and Votes Reconsidered: Congressional Elections, 1972–1982." *Public Choice*. Vol. 47, No. 1 (January): 7–62.

———. 1987. "The Marginals Never Vanished: Incumbency and Competition in Elections to the U.S. House of Representatives, 1952–1982." *American Journal of Political Science*. Vol. 31, No. 1 (February): 126–41.

———. 1990. "The Effects of Campaign Spending in House Elections: New Evidence for Old Arguments." *American Journal of Political Science*. Vol. 34, No. 2 (May): 334–62.

———. 2000a. "Party Polarization in National Politics: The Electoral Connection." In Jon R. Bond and Richard Fleisher, eds., *Polarized Politics*. Washington, DC: CQ Press: 9–30.

———. 2000b. "Reversal of Fortune: The Transformation of U.S. House Elections in the 1990s." In David W. Brady, John F. Cogan, and Morris Fiorina, eds., *Continuity and Change in House Elections*. Stanford, CA: Stanford University Press: 10–38.

————. 2001. *The Politics of Congressional Elections*, 5th ed. New York: Longman.

————. 2003. "Party Polarization in Presidential Support: The Electoral Connection." *Congress and the Presidency*. Vol. 30, No. 1 (Spring): 1–36.

————. 2004. *The Politics of Congressional Elections*, 6th ed. New York: Longman.

————. 2007. *A Divider, Not a Uniter: George W. Bush and the American People*. New York: Pearson Longman.

James, Scott C. 2000. *Presidents, Parties and the State: A Party System Perspective on Democratic Regulatory Choice, 1884–1936*. New York: Cambridge University Press.

Janda, Kenneth, Jeffrey M. Berry, and Jerry Goldman. 2005. *The Challenge of Democracy*. Boston: Houghton Mifflin.

Jewell, Malcolm E., and David A. Breaux. 1988. "The Effect of Incumbency on State Legislative Elections." *Legislative Studies Quarterly*. Vol. 13, No. 4 (November): 495–514.

Johannes, John R. 1979. "Casework as a Technique of U.S. Congressional Oversight of the Executive." *Legislative Studies Quarterly*. Vol. 4, No. 3 (August): 325–51.

Johannes, John R., and John C. McAdams. 1981. "The Congressional Incumbency Effect: Is It Casework, Policy Compatibility, or Something Else?" *American Journal of Political Science*. Vol. 25, No. 3 (August): 512–42.

Jones, Charles O. 1959. "Secular Realignment and the Party System." *Journal of Politics*. Vol. 21, No. 2 (May): 198–210.

———— 1964. "Inter-party Competition in Congressional Seats." *Western Political Quarterly*. Vol. 17, No. 3 (September): 461–76.

Key, V. O. 1959. "Secular Realignment and the Party System." *Journal of Politics*. Vol. 21, No. 2 (May): 198–210.

Krasno, Jonathon S., and Donald P. Green. 1988. "Preempting Quality Challengers in House Elections." *Journal of Politics*. Vol. 50, No. 4 (November): 920–36.

Krehbiel, Keith, and John R. Wright. 1983. "The Incumbency Effect in Congressional Elections: A Test of Two Explanations." *American Journal of Political Science*. Vol. 27, No. 1 (February): 140–57.

Leogrande, William M., and Alana S. Jeydel. 1997. "Using Presidential Election Returns to Measure Constituency Ideology: A Research Note." *American Politics Quarterly*. Vol. 25, No. 1 (January): 3–18.

Levitt, Steven D., and Catherine D. Wolfram. 1997. "Decomposing the Sources of Incumbency Advantage." *Legislative Studies Quarterly*. Vol. 22, No. 1 (February): 45–60.

MacRae, Duncan, Jr. 1952. "The Relation between Roll Call Votes and Constituencies in the Massachusetts House of Representatives." *American Political Science Review*. Vol. 46, No. 4 (December): 1046–55.

Mann, Thomas E. 1978. *Unsafe at Any Margin*. Washington, DC: American Enterprise Institute.

Martis, Kenneth C. 1982. *The Historical Atlas of United States Congressional Districts, 1789–1983*. New York: Free Press.

Mayhew, David R. 1966. *Party Loyalty among Congressmen*. Cambridge, MA: Harvard University Press.

———. 1974a. "Congressional Elections: The Case of the Vanishing Marginals." *Polity*. Vol. 6, No. 3 (Spring): 295–317.

———. 1974b. *The Electoral Connection*. New Haven, CT: Yale University Press.

———. 2002. *Electoral Realignments: A Critique of an American Genre*. New Haven, CT: Yale University Press.

McAdams, John C., and John R. Johannes. 1988. "Congressmen, Perquisites, and Elections." *Journal of Politics*. Vol. 50, No. 2 (May): 412–39.

Menefee-Libey, David. 2000. *The Triumph of Candidate-Centered Politics*. New York: Chatham House.

Nelson, Candice J. 1978–1979. "The Effect of Incumbency on Voting in Congressional Elections." *Political Science Quarterly*. Vol. 93, No. 4 (Winter): 665–78.

Nie, Norman, Sidney Verba, and John Petrocik. 1976. *The Changing American Voter*. Cambridge, MA: Harvard University Press.

Parker, Glenn R. 1980. "The Advantage of Incumbency in House Elections." *American Politics Quarterly*. Vol. 8, No. 4 (October): 375–98.

Patterson, Thomas E. 2006. *We the People: A Concise Introduction to American Politics*, 6th ed. New York: McGraw-Hill.

Payne, James L. 1980. "The Personal Electoral Advantage of House Incumbents, 1936–1976." *American Politics Research*. Vol. 8, No. 4 (October): 465–482.

Perlstein, Rick. 2001. *Before the Storm: Barry Goldwater and the Unmaking of the American Consensus*. New York: Hill and Wang.

Phillips, Kevin. 1969. *The Emerging Republican Majority*. New York: Anchor.

Polsby, Nelson W. 1968. "The Institutionalization of the U.S. House of Representatives." *American Political Science Review*. Vol. 62, No. 1 (March): 144–68.

———. 2004. *How Congress Evolves: Social Bases of Institutional Change*. New York: Oxford University Press.

Poole, Keith T., and Howard Rosenthal. 1984. "The Polarization of American Politics." *Journal of Politics*. Vol. 46, No. 4 (November): 1061–79.

———. 1985. "A Spatial Model for Legislative Roll Call Analysis." *American Journal of Political Science*. Vol. 29, No. 2 (May): 357–84.

———. 1991. "Patterns of Congressional Voting." *American Journal of Political Science*. Vol. 35, No. 1 (February): 228–78.

———. 1997. *Congress: A Political-Economic History of Roll Call Voting.* New York: Oxford University Press.

Rae, Nicol C. 1989. *The Decline and Fall of the Liberal Republicans from 1952 to the Present.* New York: Oxford University Press.

Sanders, Elizabeth. 1999. *Roots of Reform: Farmers, Workers, and the American State.* Chicago: University of Chicago Press.

Schwarz, John E., and Barton Fenmore. 1977. "Presidential Election Results and Congressional Roll Call Behavior: The Cases of 1964, 1968, and 1972." *Legislative Studies Quarterly*. Vol. 2, No. 4 (November): 409–22.

Serra, George. 1994. "What's in It for Me: The Impact of Congressional Casework on Incumbent Evaluation." *American Politics Quarterly*. Vol. 22, No. 4 (October): 403–20.

Serra, George, and Albert D. Cover. 1992. "The Electoral Consequences of Perquisite Use: The Casework Case." *Legislative Studies Quarterly*. Vol. 17, No. 2 (May): 233–46.

Shea, Daniel M., Joanne Connor Green, and Christopher E. Smith. 2007. *Living Democracy.* Upper Saddle River, NJ: Prentice Hall.

Sinclair, Barbara. 1982. *Congressional Realignment 1925–1978.* Austin: University of Texas Press.

Stimson, James A. 2005. *Tides of Consent: How Public Opinion Shapes American Politics.* New York: Cambridge University Press.

Stonecash, Jeffrey M. 2003. "Reconsidering the Trend in Incumbent Vote Percentages in House Elections." *American Review of Politics*. Vol. 24, No. 1 (Fall): 225–39.

———. 2005. *Parties Matter: Realignment and the Return of Partisanship.* Boulder, CO: Lynne Rienner.

———. 2007. "The Rise of Conservatives: More Conservatives or More Concentrated Conservatives?" In John Green, ed., *The State of the Parties*, 5th ed. Boulder, CO: Rowman and Littlefield: 317–330.

Stonecash, Jeffrey M., Mark D. Brewer, and Mack D. Mariani. 2003. *Diverging Parties: Social Change, Realignment, and Party Polarization.* Boulder, CO: Westview.

Stonecash, Jeffrey M., and Nicole R. Lindstrom. 1999. "Emerging Party Cleavages in the House of Representatives: 1962–1996." *American Politics Quarterly*. Vol. 27, No. 1 (January): 58–88.

Sundquist, James L. 1983. *Dynamics of the Party System: Alignment and Realignment of Political Parties in the United States*, rev. ed. Washington, DC: The Brookings Institution.

Tufte, Edward R. 1973. "The Relationship between Seats and Votes in Two-Party Systems." *American Political Science Review*. Vol. 67, No. 2 (June): 540–54.

Turner, Julius. 1951. *Party and Constituency: Pressures on Congress.* Baltimore: Johns Hopkins University Press.

Turner, Julius, and Edward V. Schneier. 1970. *Party and Constituency: Pressures on Congress*, rev. ed. Baltimore: Johns Hopkins University Press.

Ware, Alan. 2006. *The Democratic Party Moves North: 1877–1962*. New York: Cambridge University Press.

Wattenberg, Martin P. 1991. *The Rise of Candidate-Centered Politics: Presidential Elections of the 1980s*. Cambridge, MA: Harvard University Press.

Wilson, James Q., and John J. Dilulio Jr. 2006. *American Government: The Essentials*. Boston: Houghton Mifflin.

Yiannakis, Diana Evans. 1981. "The Grateful Electorate: Casework and Congressional Elections." *American Journal of Political Science*. Vol. 25, No. 3 (August): 568–80.

Zaller, John R. 1992. *The Nature and Origins of Mass Opinion*. New York: Cambridge University Press.

Index